Young and Old
Together

Carol Seefeldt and Barbara Warman
with Richard K. Jantz and Alice Galper

National Association for the Education of Young Children
Washington, D.C.

Photo credits: *Cover*—Dena Bawinkel; *p. 3*—Nancy P. Alexander; *p. 7*—© Sandee Soloway; *p. 12*—Francis Wardle; *p. 20*—Roger W. Neal; *p. 27*—© Hildegard Adler; *p. 33*—Blakely Fetridge Bundy; *p. 38*—R. Meier; *p. 43*—Cheryl Namkung; *p. 47*—© Florence Sharp; *p. 50*—Becky Adler

National Association for the Education of Young Children
1834 Connecticut Ave., N.W.
Washington, DC 20009-5786

The National Association for the Education of Young Children attempts through its publications program to provide a forum for discussion of major issues and ideas in our field. We hope to provoke thought and promote professional growth. The views expressed or implied are not necessarily those of the Association.

Library of Congress Catalog Card Number: 90-061183

ISBN: 0-935989-34-X

NAEYC #347

Design and production: Jack Zibulsky

Printed in the United States of America.

Contents

Acknowledgments

This manual is based on more than a decade of research on intergenerational attitudes. We gratefully acknowledge the contributions of Dr. Sue Bredekamp, Director of Professional Development, National Association for the Education of Young Children, and Dr. Kathy Serock, Contract Facilitator, Children's Services Council of Palm Beach County, Florida, who as graduate students assisted in the development and research on children's attitudes toward the elderly and elders' attitudes toward children.

Appreciation is expressed to the children of the Charles County and Prince George's County public schools who participated in the research and to their teachers who supported and guided our research. Sincere thanks are also given to the many elder volunteers who originally contributed to the ideas in this manual and who continue to work to improve the quality of life for today's young children.

About the Authors

Carol Seefeldt is a Professor at the Institute for Child Study, University of Maryland, where she teaches graduate and undergraduate classes. She received the Distinguished Scholar–Teacher Award from the University for 1983–1984. During her 35 years in the field of education she has taught at every level from nursery school through the third grade. In Florida, Carol was a Regional Training Officer for Project Head Start and conducted training programs for Head Start teachers and teachers of migrant children. Her research interests have revolved around curriculum for young children, children's attitudes toward the elderly and elders' attitudes toward children.

Barbara Warman received her Masters of Education from the University of Maryland's Institute for Child Study where she served as a research assistant. She has been involved in the development of intergenerational programs, counseling parents about child–care concerns, and working with child–care providers to facilitate parent–staff communication. She is married and has two young children, Gwen and Sam.

Richard K. Jantz, Professor of Curriculum and Instruction at the University of Maryland, teaches graduate and undergraduate classes in social studies education. He received the Distinguished Major Professor Award from the Association of Teacher Educators in 1986 and was named the outstanding academic advisor in the Division of Human and Community Resources at the University in 1984. He is active in the American Association of Colleges for Teacher Education and the National Council for Accreditation of Teacher Education. His research has focused on the study of children's attitudes toward the elderly and elders' attitudes toward children.

Alice Galper has been Chairperson and Associate Professor of the Department of Human Development/Childhood Education at Mount Vernon College in Washington, D.C. since 1983. Her long-standing research interest has been in facilitating contacts between young and old and in assisting individuals in developing more positive views of the aging process and their own aging. Alice has participated in numerous conferences discussing the application of classroom knowledge to internship settings.

Introduction

In the United States, historic numbers of people now live well into old age, and thus the percentage of the population over age 65 is steadily increasing. How society meets the challenges of an aging population begins with how today's young children learn about the elderly and about their own aging. Young children are decidedly ambivalent about the elderly. On the one hand, children seem to have deep affection for older people, especially their grandparents, whom they love dearly. They also think that old people are generally good and quite probably rich. "They have money to take you places and buy you neat things," a first grader remarked. On the other hand, children do not want to be with, or do things with, old people. They are appalled by the physical aspects of old age. Children loath the wrinkles and physical disabilities of the old. They shudder as they explain that elderly people "chew funny," "walk with canes," "need glasses to see and can't hear too well either," or that "old people just sit all day in wheelchairs waiting to die" (Jantz, Seefeldt, Galper, & Serock, 1976).

Moreover, children are clear about their feelings of growing old: It won't happen to them. When children between the ages of three and 11 were asked how they felt about their own aging and being old, they simply denied the fact: "Oh no, not me! I'm not getting old." "You see," one child explained, "you have a better chance of not dying if you are brand new." Another answered, "I'm not getting old because then the joy of life will be gone" (Seefeldt, 1977).

These negative attitudes are potentially harmful. Like any biases, they limit thinking and, often, behavior. Children who perceive the old as sick, unable to do anything, and in the least productive time of life may dread their own aging. Their stereotypical thinking may affect how they, as adults, decide to provide and care for the elderly.

Stereotyping the old could also lead to conflict between young and old. Some predict that because the old are now the richest, most powerful lobbying group in our country, and children the nation's most impoverished and neglected group, it is only a matter of time before open antagonism results between those who advocate for young and old. Our nation cannot tolerate divisiveness between interest groups for the young and old, nor can a society flourish without individuals whose lives are satisfying and fulfilling at every age.

Ways must be found to help children understand and accept their own aging and develop positive feelings toward the elderly. Because children's school experiences affect how they view these subjects, educators have a responsibility to examine how they influence children's attitudes and knowledge of aging and the old. Teachers can plan systematic ways to foster the development of positive attitudes. Through curriculum experiences, organized contact with the old, and the school's resources, children can learn:

- that each age and stage of life is full of unique potential
- to live fully each moment of each day of their lives
- to think creatively and with flexibility, meeting the challenges of today in order to meet those of the future
- to question stereotypical thinking about age and the elderly
- that the elderly population is a diverse group, made of individuals with a variety of characteristics
- how to relate to, care for, and cooperate and share with others

Children who have the opportunity to live fully today will not dread their own aging. Robert Butler writes that when people have tasted all the life cycle has to offer, they accept "the basic fairness of each generation's taking its turn on the face of the planet" (1975, p. 422). Children who learn, when young, the skills of relating to and caring for one another may become adults who find flexible, creative ways of caring for the elderly. If today's children are able to free themselves from the myths and stereotypes of age, they can enjoy a society in which young and old together successfully meet the challenges of the coming "senior boom."

This manual is for teachers of young children ages three to eight and for administrators of child care, nursery, or preschool programs who are planning an intergenerational program. It lays out guidelines for planning curriculum experiences (Part One), developing programs that establish and maintain contact between young and old (Part Two), and selecting and using appropriate resources from the school and community (Appendixes). These guidelines were developed to achieve the following goals.

1. To provide children with accurate information and knowledge about the elderly that will enable them to form positive, realistic concepts of and attitudes toward the elderly.
2. To expose children to an unbiased look at the diversity of old people, teaching them to value the many, varied characteristics, attributes, and qualities of the elderly.
3. To enable children to feel positively about their own aging and about the elderly.

Intergenerational Curriculum for Young Children

Teaching active, impulsive, adventurous children, who are intent on the "here and now," about aging and the elderly may seem a difficult task. Concepts of aging are highly complex and difficult to understand at any age. Therefore, knowing how children think and feel about aging and the elderly, understanding how to plan developmentally appropriate curriculum experiences, and using effective teaching strategies are necessary in the complicated process of teaching about these subjects.

Being developmentally appropriate _____

All of the curriculum experiences children have with aging and the elderly must be developmentally appropriate. Because of the need to match curriculum to the ways all children learn and to the maturational level of each individual child, the curriculum will be one of action, consider children's feelings, and use effective teaching strategies.

Providing active learning

Children are doers; learning is really a do-it-yourself project for them. Without doing, without experiencing for themselves, little learning occurs. Acting on the environment—pulling, pushing, touching, messing around—and interacting with others give children the

1

materials required for thinking. It is only through firsthand experiences that children obtain the material necessary for them to categorize, reflect, and draw relationships and conclusions about aging and the elderly.

Classrooms, whether in a child care center, nursery school, public school kindergarten, or primary grade, will have a wide variety of materials for children's firsthand learning. Centers of interest, including library, arts and crafts, blocks, music, math, and science areas, are essential. The science area, complete with living things—plants, insects, fish, reptiles, small mammals—for children to observe, chart, and record the life cycle, fosters children's concepts of aging. Art and music areas give children the opportunity to use materials to express their own feelings, ideas, and concepts of aging and the elderly. The library area could contain reference materials on aging and the elderly and poetry, short stories, and books featuring older characters.

People of all ages are a part of an active classroom. When older people are regularly and continually involved in classroom activities, interactions between young and old occur naturally. Older people might visit only once to provide a special program or to assist with a school function, or they may be paid aides or regular volunteers.

It is important that children's experiences with elders do not serve to confirm their stereotyped view of the old as sick, tired, and infirm. Elders who represent the wide range of physical characteristics and the variety of individual characteristics of all people should be involved in the curriculum and classroom.

Basic integrity is necessary when providing contact between young and old. In a second grade classroom, the children did not see a 91-year-old man who was in a wheelchair as infirm. They admired his mental alertness, sense of humor, and ability to teach the class Spanish.

On the other hand, young children seem to be afraid of elders who are infirm both physically and mentally. Because children are trying "to figure out what are the essential attributes of their own selfhood, what aspects of self remain constant" (Derman-Sparks, 1989, p. 2), they worry that they can somehow catch infirmities from old people or suddenly become old themselves. "If I touch her will I catch it?" asked a three year-old who was taken to visit an infirm woman who had to be restrained in a wheelchair in the nursing home.

The same confusion over what aspects of self remain constant may be why children are afraid of growing old themselves. Children worry that they will not be the same person if they grow old, or that they could suddenly turn into an old person when they have a birthday or if they misbehave. One almost-three-year-old told her grandmother she was not going to have a birthday party when she was three. Her sur-

2

prised grandmother asked why and was told, "I don't want to be three, I want to stay me."

Curriculum about aging is built through firsthand experiences with elders who have different characteristics, skills, abilities, and a wide variety of physical characteristics, as well as with children's own growth and aging. Through contacts with the old that are positive and have integrity, and with a focus on their own growth and aging, children develop positive feelings toward age and the elderly, and increase their knowledge of aging and the old.

When older people are regularly and continually involved in classroom activities, interactions between young and old occur naturally.

Considering feelings

Feelings underlie all learning. Children's beliefs and attitudes about their own aging and the elderly stem from their feelings. For example, one child felt afraid of the elderly because she knew only of the wicked old witch in the fairy tales she had heard. She was afraid of the witch, and her fear led her to believe that all old people were ugly and mean and could actually hurt her if they wanted.

How children feel about themselves, in part, determines how they will feel about others. Children who are insecure and uncomfortable with themselves are likely to feel insecure about their own aging. This insecurity can lead to difficulty in adjusting to the changes aging brings, as well as in relating to others who are both older and younger than they. Secure children, comfortable with themselves, can adjust to change and will be able to establish new patterns of behavior as they themselves grow, change, and age.

To foster children's security, encourage them to talk about and express their feelings in many ways. Let them initiate their own activities, give them responsibilities commensurate with their capabilities, and allow them to experience success.

Teaching attitudes

Some say children's attitudes are caught rather than taught. Research suggests that children learn some of their attitudes toward the elderly through identification with and imitation of people who are important to them. Because teachers are very important to young children, it is crucial for teachers to demonstrate positive attitudes toward their own aging and the elderly. In examining your own attitudes, you might ask:

- What older people do I know?
- What do I do with them?
- How do I really feel about them?
- How do I really feel about growing old myself?
- What facts do I know about growing old and the elderly?
- Do I make jokes about my age?
- What language do I use to describe aging and the elderly?
- Where did I learn to think as I do?

Learning the facts about aging and recognizing ageism in our society can begin with this type of self-examination. The many useful books, articles, films, and organizations listed in the appendixes will help you explore your own attitudes and feelings on this subject. Knowledge of your own attitudes toward aging and the elderly, and knowledge about the facts, permits you to challenge children's stereotypes. With self-knowledge and understanding you can directly and matter-of-factly confront children when they reveal stereotypes about the elderly. Derman-Sparks (1989) suggests that, rather than ignoring children's asking about differences between young and old, you do not change the subject, but answer and respond as directly as possible (NAEYC's *Anti-Bias Curriculum,* Derman-Sparks, 1989, contains other useful suggestions).

Involving parents

Parents are probably more significant influences on children's attitudes on aging than teachers and need to be involved in the curriculum. For example, a newsletter could explain a few of the curriculum's goals and how parents could help work toward them. From time to time, it could describe activities and experiences the children have in the intergenerational program.

The best way to involve parents in the curriculum, however, is for them to help out in school activities. For instance, they could join children on a field trip. They can arrange to take their own children to visit older relatives or friends, show children photo albums depicting the lives of grandparents or great grandparents, and take part in family reunions. Parents whose older relatives live nearby or with them may be particularly good resources for helping all children confront their biases.

Integrating the curriculum

Curriculum that fosters positive attitudes toward age and the elderly is part of the whole life of the school. You may carefully plan projects developed around specific goals that would occur throughout the day, month, or year. Most often, however, the curriculum on aging and the elderly is integrated into the rest of the curriculum.

Children learn as they live. You can use all of the incidental, spontaneous happenings that occur through the day to help children understand their own aging and to develop positive attitudes toward the elderly. Being able to recognize the teachable moment, and knowing how to use it, is possible when you are clear on your teaching objectives. Observing an older person attempting to cross a busy intersection while children are on a walking field trip, a surprise visit by a child's grandparent, the birth of a new baby, or a child's new accomplishment can all be used to increase children's knowledge at the moment, or to introduce a more formal lesson about growth and growing old.

Planning for three- and four-year-olds _____

Characteristics of threes and fours

"I'm three!" proclaims a child holding up three fingers to make sure you know exactly how old she is. Three- and four-year-olds do know how old they are and are interested in waiting for and having a birthday. They enjoy their own parties and anticipate the parties of others. These very young children also enjoy reliving their babyhood, looking at baby pictures, and listening to stories about when they were a baby. And they are also ready to think about tomorrow, when they will be bigger, and what they will do when they go to kindergarten. As they are barely in the preoperational stage of thinking, their overall sense of time is very meager. Their thinking and learning is truly dependent on the "here and now."

Nevertheless, preschoolers do use symbols. They have the vocabulary to communicate effectively, and they love to play with language. The sounds and patterns of language found in folk tales, poetry, stories, or even their own silly chants and songs intrigue. Fours are interested in stories and able to listen to them in small groups and even to discuss them with an adult or another child. They also show traces of using symbols in their artwork. Beginning representation occurs in their scribbles and paintings, with a circle used to stand for a person, or a square for a house.

Knowledge of age and the elderly. As would be expected, three- and four-year-olds have limited knowledge of these subjects. They tend to confuse concepts of age and size, believing, for example, that their mother and grandmother are the same age because they are the same size. They also think they will catch up with a child two years older, or that they will grow older but their grandmother will stay the same age because she stays the same size. In addition, threes and fours believe that people grow older at different rates, or that they may grow old very suddenly. Aging could happen to them, for instance, if some specific event occurred, perhaps an illness or accident, or even being with an older person. Finally, preschoolers have limited concepts of number and age. They say a 40-year-old man is about three, or an 80-year-old man is "maybe 10 years old."

6

*Through positive firsthand experiences with elders,
children develop warm attitudes and accurate concepts.*

7

Attitudes about age and the elderly. At no other age are attitudes toward age and the elderly expressed so openly and so negatively. Even though they say they love their grandparents, and seem to have positive affect for some old people, preschoolers say they prefer to be with younger people rather than older; believe that old people are sick, ugly, and bad; and deny that they will grow old. They say they would feel "very bad" if they were old.

Goals, objectives, and activities

GOAL 1

To provide accurate information and knowledge about the elderly.

OBJECTIVE: *To involve the elderly in the classroom to acquaint children with a variety of older people.*

Invite an older neighbor, an older staff member, or a child's grandparent to visit the class frequently. Once the older person and the children are familiar with one another, the elder might:

- Read a story to one or two children, holding them on his lap.
- Read poems from *Children of Long Ago* (Little, 1988). These are likely to remind the elder of stories of his childhood or his parents' and grandparents' childhood. Children can see that in many ways their childhood is very much the same as the elder's.
- Take part in a birthday party for a child and show the children how many candles she would need on her birthday cake or tell what she remembers from her third or fourth birthday. She could tell the children how birthdays and holidays were celebrated when she was little.
- Play with the children, helping them with their activities.
- Help prepare a special snack with the children, perhaps something he enjoyed eating when he was a child.
- Entertain with a special activity. Perhaps a group of elderly could sing (a barbershop quartet) or dance (a square dance club).
- Discuss with children the things they do for their grandparents and the things their grandparents do for them.

GOAL 2

To expose children to an unbiased look at the diversity of old people.

OBJECTIVE: *To teach them to value the many and varied characteristics, attributes, and qualities of the elderly.*

- When possible, ask children's grandparents to visit the class. During the visits, you can discuss how grandparents are alike and how they differ. Some may have gray hair, others black hair. How grandparents are alike and different can be pointed out.
- Make special cards for grandparents or an older volunteer during holiday celebrations. Have the children dictate their greeting, discuss how the grandparents are different yet alike.
- Read *Grandma and Grandpa* (Oxenbury, 1984) and discuss with the children the things they do with their grandparents. Also, read *Annie's Four Grannies* (Kross, 1986) or *I Dance in My Red Pajamas* (Hurd, 1982). These stories are particularly good for preschoolers because they convey the feeling that older people can be fun and interesting. These books also show the diversity of older persons, and their similarities, for in both books grandparents and children pretend, have fun and help one another.

GOAL 3

To enable children to feel positively about their own aging and the elderly.

OBJECTIVE: *To focus on children's aging and to develop the concept of growth and development.*

- Read *When You Were a Baby* (Jonas, 1982) or another book that illustrates what babies do.
- Have children bring in baby clothes or toys they or their siblings used and discuss during show-and-tell. Let them share what they know about these objects by using them during play. For instance, they might demonstrate how babies use the toys or the baby bottle. If this pretend play gets too rambunctious, turn on lullaby music so the "babies" can take a nap. The baby

props should be added to the housekeeping area as they permit and encourage children to think about their own history and babyhood. It's comforting for preschoolers to know how big they are now and to know it's still safe to be a baby who is cared for and loved.

- Have parents bring in snapshots of the children as infants and as toddlers, along with a current snapshot. Through discussions, the children can see that they are still the same person, but that they have grown and developed. A book that helps children understand their growing up is *It's My Birthday* (Watanabe, 1988), in which a bear looks at snapshots from his birthday parties and other special growing up occasions.

- Hold simple birthday celebrations for the children as they turn three or four. Make a badge or sign with a large numeral 3 or 4 for the birthday child to wear. Have children decorate cookies or cupcakes for the celebration by putting only three raisins, nuts, or pieces of fruit on each.

- Read *The Growing Story* (Krauss, 1947). Ask children how they are just like the boy in the story. Have they ever outgrown any clothes? What did they do with them? Compare a pair of baby shoes or booties with a pair of children's shoes, or compare a baby sweater with the sweaters the children are wearing. How have the children changed? Ask, "Will you ever outgrow the shoes or sweater you are wearing today? How does it feel to grow older?" Also, you could read *You'll Soon Grow Into Them* (Hutchins, 1983) or *Titch* (Hutchins, 1971). These books open the way for other discussions about growth.

- During circle time, use music, rhymes, and finger plays that focus on babies and growing. Children will enjoy "Rock a Bye Baby," "Pat a Cake," and other familiar Mother Goose rhymes and songs. Ask them if they remember these rhymes and why they think babies like them so much. Appendix A lists books that have rhymes and fingerplays, and records and tapes that set them to music. Be sure to send home copies of any new rhymes so parents can share in this activity.

- Have children observe plants growing, developing, and changing. Plant some seeds that will sprout quickly, such as scarlet runners and other beans, peas, or corn. Focus children's attention on the changes that occur as the seeds sprout and grow.

OBJECTIVE: *To develop children's ability to describe their feelings toward aging and the elderly.*

- Make clarifying statements as the children work and play or in connection with their activities and the experiences they have during a birthday party or a discussion of growing older. Statements such as "You must feel good about that," "I understand how you feel; you want it now," or "Yes, that would make you feel unhappy" will help children realize that they do have feelings, and that they can label these feelings and talk about them.

- Encourage children to talk about their feelings: "Tell John what you want instead of hitting. He doesn't know what you want when you hit." Or, "Wait a minute, when you scream it's hard to know what you mean. Tell me in words instead."

- Select several books portraying elderly characters. After reading the books, ask the children what they think is good about growing old and what is bad. Try to dispel myths by choosing books that depict elders in active, fulfilled roles. (See Appendix A for suggestions.)

- Ask an older person to give a firsthand account of growing old. Ask the children what they want to know about growing older, and make a list of questions to ask the person.

- Relate the children's feelings to the feelings of others: "I can tell she's happy—look at her smile." "How do you think he feels about that?" "Did your grandmother feel happy when you showed her your painting?"

- Make special cards for grandparents or for older volunteers at holiday times. Have each child dictate a sentence for the card telling how she feels about the older person. Fours like to paste bits of colored paper on the front of the cards for decoration.

Planning for five-year-olds _____

Characteristics of fives

Fives are really alive—alive with curiosity about everything in their world and beyond. A bit surer of themselves than fours, five-year-olds are secure and calm. They try only what they think they can accomplish and therefore often accomplish what they try.

Five-year-olds are friendly. They enjoy the company of people of all ages. Because they are more in control of themselves, they're not too

*Introducing children to artifacts from earlier ways of
life fosters interest in and understanding of older people.*

demanding of others. Kindergartners work well in groups and enjoy group games and activities. They appreciate and enjoy stories and poems, so plan group discussions and activities based on literature.

Five-year-olds can count with one-to-one correspondence to 10, recognize and use numerals, and understand simple time concepts. For instance, they can make plans for tomorrow and think about things they did yesterday. They can count the days until some event, or the days that have passed since the event.

Understanding of aging and knowledge of the elderly. Five-year-olds are still confused about age/time concepts. They seem to worry that they could suddenly grow old or might even "catch" wrinkles and the physical characteristics of age themselves. Kindergartners report having limited contact and interaction with older people and are unable to think of any other names for the elderly besides "old people."

Some fives appear to understand the progression of aging. Nearly half of a sample of five-year-olds were able to put pictures of a man portrayed at four stages of life in order from the youngest to oldest (Galper, Seefeldt, Jantz, & Serock, 1980). Many believe, however, that they will catch up to an older person in age, that they will grow but the other person will stay the same age. Talking about a cousin who had come to live with his family, José said, "Juanita is 10 years older than I am. In 10 years I'll be as old as Juanita."

Time and age are associated strongly in children's minds with size and space. The larger the person, the older he must be. People who are about the same size must be about the same age. Children believe that age differences might be annulled or reversed by growth in height. One five said, "I could get older than her when I get bigger."

Attitudes about the elderly and aging. Like three- and four-year-olds, fives are very negative about their aging and about the elderly. They seem concerned that they will not be the same person if they grow old. They assign the characteristics of sick, ugly, bad, and rich to older people and are appalled by the physical signs of aging. They see the changes in mobility, vision, and hearing, and hair loss and wrinkles, which none of us likes very much, as most detrimental and even fear these changes. Fives report that they prefer to be with younger rather than older people because they can do more fun things with younger people.

Goals, objectives, and activities

GOAL 1

To provide accurate information and knowledge about the elderly.

OBJECTIVE: *To acquaint children with a variety of elderly people in a diversity of lifestyles.*

- Invite a number of elderly people to participate in classroom activities. Ask them to tell, or show, the children how their mother washed clothes, where they got their news, what games they played, the kind of house they lived in, and so forth. At other times, these volunteers could show children how to make something they learned to make when they were children — perhaps a God's Eye, cat's cradle, or clay beads. They could demonstrate weaving, quilting, or modeling with clay.
- Collect a number of tapes of the children's grandparents, old people in the neighborhood, or elderly friends. Have these people tape a folk tale or tell a story of when they were little. Children can listen to these tapes at a listening station during activity time or take them home.
- Ask children to find out what type of home their grandparents have. Do they live in an apartment building, a single-family home, an extended-care facility? Make a list of the different types of places people live. Have children find out what their grandparents do, their favorite hobbies, the things they enjoy doing the most, and those they don't like at all.

OBJECTIVE: *To develop the concept that all people are similar in many ways, even though they may be of different ages and have different characteristics.*

Since children are always eager to play, the focus of these activities is on play and recreation as lifelong endeavors. Children will discover that the old have had similar play experiences in their lifetime and that people of all ages enjoy similar activities.

- Read *Children of Long Ago* (Little, 1988). Then make a class list of favorite games and things to do. Are these things the same as or different from things children used to play long ago? Talk about recreation as a lifelong occurrence. Send the children's list home so parents can tell about their favorite games and play activities in their childhood and nowadays.

- Ask older volunteers or parents to share some of the fun things they used to do as children and those they do for fun now. Read about Appalachian toys, for instance, which older people played with and still make for children. *The Foxfire Book, Volume 6* (Wigginton, 1980) describes these toys and how to make them. The children could make some, or volunteers could demonstrate making them to the class.
- Try to have available some toys and games that both children and old people are familiar with and enjoy. You or an older person can teach children how to play jacks, marbles, checkers, cards, or kick-the-can, and how to fly a kite or roll hoops.
- Have an older person assist in teaching children some simple square dance moves. Recruit a square dance caller to come to parents' night or some other school function that includes adults. Let the children demonstrate their skills and then invite the parents and grandparents to join in for a hoe-down.
- Discuss with the children how they are like their parents and grandparents. What do they like to do with their parents or grandparents? Do they believe they will become parents some day? How will mother feel when she is a grandmother? Have children dictate stories about what kind of parents they will be when they grow up.
- Ask children to name their favorite foods. Have them find out their parents' and grandparents' favorite foods. Have children cut pictures of food out of newspapers and magazines to make a scrapbook of their favorite foods, or a chart for the room. On a large sheet of brown wrapping paper, make three columns labeled: Foods We Like, Foods Our Parents Like, and Foods Our Grandparents Like. Then have children paste the pictures in the appropriate columns. Small pictures of children, parents, and grandparents let children know where to paste the pictures. Discuss similarities and differences. Children may have seen advertisements portraying adults as hiding because they are eating children's cereal. Is there really such a thing as food only for children or only for adults? Which foods are only for children and which are only for adults?

OBJECTIVE: *To understand that all people, regardless of age, share the same feelings.*

- Read *Song and Dance Man* (Ackerman, 1988). This grandfather saved his tap shoes and costumes from his vaudeville dancing days. Ask the children why they think he kept these things in a chest. What kinds of things do they save? Have the children bring something to school that they have saved and tell how they feel about the object or memory. Often children will bring stuffed animals or blankets from babyhood. In one class a number of children brought shells and rocks from their trip to a nearby beach. Other children brought birthday cards from the previous year's birthday. In addition, ask an older person to bring in some special things she has saved and talk about how she feels about these things and their memories. Discuss how part of growing and aging is remembering times from the past. Read *Wilfred Gordon McDonald Partridge* (Fox, 1985).

- Have the children make "grandmother or grandfather" chests to keep special papers and objects in. They can cover shoe boxes with colored tissue paper or colorful wallpaper scraps. Often, parents may feel that rocks, shells, and old birthday cards are just a lot of clutter. Accompany the chests with a note to parents explaining the importance of respecting the chests' contents. Rather than tossing out an object the child brings home they can ask, "Do you want to put this in your memory chest?"

- Discuss what makes people happy, angry, or sad. Read *David Was Mad* (Martin, 1963) or *Oma and Bobo* (Schwartz, 1987). In *Oma and Bobo* a stern grandmother expresses her feelings through her actions more than through words. For example, she shuts herself in her room when she is angry. Children can tell how they feel, or would feel, in a similar situation, or describe something that makes them angry. Ask an older person to tell what makes her happy, angry, or sad. Ask, "How do people share the same feelings?" "How are people's feelings different?" Give children booklets made of blank papers stapled together with the covers labeled either "Happy" or "Sad." Ask children to draw in the booklets things that make them either happy or sad.

GOAL 2

To expose children to an unbiased look at the diversity of old people.

OBJECTIVE: *To develop the concept that the elderly enjoy and participate in a variety of activities that are similar to the activities the children enjoy.*

- Read *The Berenstain Bears and the Week at Grandma's* (Berenstain & Berenstain, 1986), and ask the children to think about things they do, their parents do, and their grandparents do. Despite the heavy moral and sexist tone of the Berenstain books, this one is helpful because the grandparents do not only traditional things like baking and fishing with their grandchildren, but also nontraditional things. The grandparents also introduce the cubs to their own special interests and hobbies, and Gramps demonstrates yo-yo moves he remembers from his childhood.

- Have the children act out an activity and ask the group to guess what the activity is and whether it is done by the child, the child's parents, or the grandparents. Keep track of the activities on a chart. At the end of the game review the list and see if some of the things done by children are also done by adults and vice versa.

- Have the children, parents, and older volunteers bring in some of their favorite music for a music history day. Some participants might bring a record, and others could play an instrument, sing, or dance. Present the music chronologically, and ask the participants to tell where the music was played, what kind of dancing was done to it, and whether it was usually played by a band, or sung by an individual or a group. Be sure to end with a sing-along of songs familiar to everyone such as "Working on the Railroad," "Mary Had a Little Lamb," or "She'll Be Coming Round the Mountain." This will help children see that everyone has different tastes in and knowledge of music, but all can still enjoy music together and have musical tastes in common.

OBJECTIVE: *To develop the concept that people have similar and different characteristics.*

- Play a game in which the leader describes her characteristics one at a time. For example, the first characteristic named might be "I am a girl." Everyone who shares the characteristic stands up, so all the girls stand up. Next, the leader names another characteristic, such as "I have brown hair." Those girls who don't have brown hair would sit down, and any girls or boys with brown hair would stand up. The children must pay close attention to stand or sit at the correct times as the game continues. When the child runs out of things to say, another leader begins naming his characteristics. The teacher might like to end the game by saying, "I am a human being." Then a discussion of what makes us all alike as human beings and different as individuals can follow.

- One way we are all different is that we each have a different face. Make a learning station called "Faces." Cut out a number of pictures of people's faces. Be certain to include people of different ages, sexes, races, and cultures, as well as those with different expressions. Mount these on heavy paper or cardboard, and cover with clear plastic. Give the children empty box lids into which they can sort the pictures any way they wish. At times, the teacher may ask them to place a certain category of faces — happy, old, White, or female, for example — together in one box lid.

- Have the children look into the mirror and describe what they see. They might each draw their face on a large mural. Ask children what characteristics they have in common.

- Show the film *Free To Be . . . You and Me* (McGraw-Hill, 1974). Ask the children to list the ways people are the same and the ways they are different. Are all old people the same? Do you know any old people who use canes? Wheelchairs? Glasses? Hearing aids? Do you know old people who play tennis? Knit? Jog? Swim?

GOAL 3

To enable children to feel positive about their own aging and the elderly.

OBJECTIVE: *To develop an understanding that the child will be the same person when older.*

- With specific information on each child's birth weight and length, their current height and weight, and the heights of their parents, you can help the children learn how they have grown, and how much more they may grow, by making a growth chart. Ask them to notice how much they've grown since the last measuring. Are they still the same person? Send home a questionnaire asking parents to record their current height and, if they want to, their weight. Then give each child paper long enough to mark how tall their parents are, how tall they are now, and how tall they were when they were born. Ask them to guess where the growth marks will be when they are adults.If they want, children can decorate the chart with pictures of growing up.

- Read A. A. Milne's "The End" (1927). (This is the poem that begins "When I was one/I was just begun/When I was two. . . .") Make a Growing Up mural. On a large sheet of brown wrapping paper paint the numerals 1 through 5. Have children contribute snapshots of themselves at the various ages, or draw a picture of something they could do at each age, and paste these on the chart. Ask them if they were the same person at age one as they are now at age five.

- Using the information collected earlier on children's birth weight, fill bags with sand until they weigh about the same as the children did at birth. (Use a bathroom scale to weigh the sand.) By holding a six-pound bag of sand, for example, children gain the concept of how small they were when they were born. Weigh the children, record their current weight, and compare it to their birth weight.

- Discuss with the children other ways they've changed since they were infants. Bring in a jar of strained fruit or other strained baby food. Give each child a taste (using popsicle sticks allows each to get a taste easily). Then ask them to taste the same fruit in the form they eat it today.

- Animals grow and change too, but still remain the same animal. Make a learning station of pictures of baby animals and pictures of fully grown animals. Mount the pictures on cardboard and cover with clear plastic paper if desired. Children then match the picture of the baby animal with the picture of the fully grown animal. Color code the backs of the cards so children can check their choices.

OBJECTIVE: *To extend children's concepts of time and the passing of time to enable them to understand their own aging.*

- Gather a collection of objects with which children are familiar. These objects should represent things the children might have used when they were younger, things they use now, and things they might use in the future. The past collection might include baby rattles, bottles, booties, and diapers. The current collection might include silverware, toys, crayons, and children's clothes. The future collection could include tools, cooking

By extending the child's concept of time and the passing of time, you enable her to understand her own aging.

utensils, adult books, and maps. Ask the children to sort these objects into boxes marked "past," "present," and "future." Once children understand the activity, add new objects. This activity can be used during group time and free play.

- Have a special show-and-tell week. Encourage children to show things that they used to use, they use now, or they plan on using in the future. The group can guess to which time period the object belongs. What things belong in only one box and what things might fit into more than one box? Did their parents and grandparents use these same objects in the past? Do they think these objects will still be used in the future when they are parents and grandparents?

- Keep track of the passing of time by marking a calendar. Count the number of days until someone's birthday or a special celebration; then count the number of days that have passed since the event. Put blocks in a pile to represent the days before some event will occur. Remove one block as each day passes. When the pile of blocks is gone, the children will know it's time for the event.

- Ask the children to think about their own past. Can they remember when they first learned to drink from a cup? When did they have their last birthday? What things can they recall from their past? What don't they remember?

- Help children speculate about the future as they discuss the past. Following a field trip, holiday celebration, or other special event, children could think about the ways the event was exactly the way they thought it would be and the ways it was different. Ask them to discuss what they will do differently at the next celebration or trip, and what they would do the same way.

Planning for six-, seven-, and eight-year-olds ____

Characteristics of six-, seven-, and eight-year-olds

Primary-grade children are capable and industrious. Self-directed and self-motivated, they are eager to do and learn. They feel real involvement in school activities and approach play as a serious business. Games that involve conventional rules are their favorites. Six-, seven-, and eight-year-olds are curious about people and events, continually asking questions. They appraise and judge events happening to themselves and others.

Children of these ages have broad social interests. They like to play with others, most of the time with children of the same sex. Friendships become closer and more exacting. Primary-age children are increasingly interested in their playmates' opinion of them and because of this are self-conscious and sensitive to differences in other people. By seven, children enjoy creating and joining clubs as well as collecting and trading things.

Because of their increased thinking ability, primary-age children are developing more accurate concepts of age and time. They can use the vocabulary of time, read a calendar, and begin to tell time on a clock. They can learn to figure the length of time between given dates, think of the separation of an event from the present in mathematical terms, and construct simple timelines.

Understanding of aging and knowledge of the elderly. Like younger children, primary-grade children report limited knowledge of and contact with the elderly. They can name an older person in their family, but not outside their family, and they have limited knowledge of alternative terms for "old people." Unlike younger children, they are able to put pictures of a man portrayed at ages 20, 40, 60, and 80 in order from youngest to oldest and assign approximately accurate ages to the pictures.

Primary-age children have inaccurate concepts of age and time. They know that they or their grandmothers grow older every year based on the fact that they both have birthdays. Even through the middle grades, however, children are unable to form the logical connections necessary to deduce birth order from age differences, or age differences from the succession of births. They understand each concept individually, but they still can't view them together.

During middle childhood, age is no longer associated with height, yet children still seem unable to view age as a continuum in its own right. "I don't think it matters how tall you are, but what else you do," one fifth grader said when asked which of the pictured men was older.

Attitudes toward aging and the elderly. Primary children do not perceive being old as anything positive, but they are less negative than preschoolers in their attitudes. On the other hand, they express highly negative feelings about their own aging. Like five-year-olds, these children say they prefer to be with younger people because they can do more interesting, active things with younger people than with older people. Primary-grade children believe being old is being sad, ugly, and sick, but they also say the old are good, clean, wonderful, and right. In general, they use stereotypes to describe the physical and behavioral characteristics of being old.

Goals, objectives, and activities

GOAL 1

To provide accurate information and knowledge about the elderly.

OBJECTIVE: *To increase children's vocabulary to include alternative names for the elderly and adjectives and adverbs that describe people.*

- Make an aging dictionary or a chart of words for the room called "Words for Growing." You could include *infant, toddler, preschooler, adolescent, teen-ager, juvenile, retiree, adult,* and *senior citizen.* Discuss the meaning of each word, and encourage children to use these in creative writing and discussions.

- Explore the use of the words *young, younger, youngest, old, older,* and *oldest.* Who is the youngest in the class? In the school? Who is the oldest in the class? In the school?

- Have second or third graders examine dictionaries for definitions of *old* and *people.* Have them list people they know. Which of these people are old people? One definition of old is "having lived beyond the middle period of life." List on the board people that children know who have lived beyond the middle period of life.

- Ask children to identify an older person — one they know personally, or one they would like to know more about. Have them find out all they can about the person and then present an overview of the person's life to the class. Children could write the story of this person's life to put into a class booklet titled "People We Know."

- Ask children to find out the difference between the words *older* and *elder* (the latter applies only to people). List things that could be old and people they know who are old . An elder is defined as "a person occupying any office requiring the dignity that age confers." Whom do the children know who fits that definition?

- Make a list of all the older people the class knows. Find out how old the people are, where they live, and what they do. Have the children draw conclusions about how older people are alike and how they are different.

OBJECTIVE: *To acquaint children with a variety of older people in a diversity of roles.*

- Invite an older person to the class to teach a traditional game. Children could discuss the rules of the game, and the visitor could tell how she used to play the game when she was young— whom she played with and the rules they followed.

- Capitalize on the children's industrious drive and arrange for them to construct some item for the classroom under the direction of an older person. It could be a rabbit hutch, new play house, piece of outdoor equipment, or bookshelf, for example.

- Ask an older person to come to the class and talk about her career. Ask how the career would be different today. Would she do the same thing again? How could she do it differently? Have the children interview their parents and grandparents and make a list of the careers represented in these groups. How many different careers do the children know about? What careers will the children select when they are adults?

- Your local senior center, Lions Club, or other service organization with elder members may have a community project that children can work on with the elders. A representative from the group could tell the children about the project. It could be anything from planting a garden for a community shelter to making signs for a charity event. The group may have specific things in mind that the children can do, or they may ask the children to come up with ideas. Bringing old and young together in a community project shows the children what an important role in the community older people have.

- Make each child a scrapbook called "People." Have children cut pictures of people from magazines and arrange them in their scrapbooks from the youngest to the oldest, or in groups based on what the people are doing. How many different things do they find older people doing? Have *People* (Spier, 1980) available for browsing.

- Third graders can invite guest speakers to give an informal presentation on a topic of interest to the class. Hobby groups are likely to have some very enthusiastic members with fascinating collections. Survey the class interests and then look for some older volunteers to come in with their insect collection, model trains, rocks, shells, or whatever the class would like to see. Let the children decide what special topics they would like to cover and let them be as involved as possible in planning the day. Children can plan for and bring refreshments, send out invitations if parents are invited, and help set up the room for the speakers. After the event they can write thank you notes. If the visitor is from a hobby club, be sure that the club member lets the children know of any public events their club is sponsoring. If the children are very enthusiastic, perhaps the volunteer would arrange a special meeting where the children could see more of the club's collections and meet more older people. *I Know a Lady* (Zolotow, 1984) is an interesting book to follow up these activities.

- Have children find an older person in their community and interview him about: the different places he has been; the kinds of work he has done; the things he is doing now; and the things he collects.

    Most of the children will still be a bit too young to do a thorough oral history, but advanced third graders may find helpful the free *Golden Days: An Oral History Guide* (Blaustein, 1985). If children are not ready to use the entire guide, choose some of the excellent questions to give to the children as they interview elders. Divide the children into groups and have them tell each other about the people they interviewed. Then ask them to talk about friendships they have had with older people and how friendship with an older person is different from friendship with a younger person. What interests do they share with the person they interviewed or with some of the other older people presented? Perhaps they would like to invite one of these people as a class presenter.

- Family units differ today. Children may have all combinations of grandparents and step-grandparents as a result of today's blended families. Ask children to make a chart of all their grandparents and great grandparents and then compare charts.

GOAL 2

To expose children to an unbiased look at the diversity of old people.

OBJECTIVE: *To explore the different ways people of different ages interact.*

- Read books and show films or videotapes that depict children in a variety of life situations with older people . The selection of books and audio-visual materials should represent a balance. For example, *Happy Birthday Grampie* (Pearson, 1987) describes the relationship between a girl and her blind grandfather who has forgotten English. The child finds a way to communicate with her grandfather in a special way. In *I Dance in My Red Pajamas* (Hurd, 1982), the grandparents are very lively, and the girl is involved in activities with both of them. *Georgia Music* (Griffith, 1986) shows a city girl learning many things as she spends the summer with her grandfather in rural Georgia. Their relationship is so special that when he needs some cheering up, she knows just how to do it.

The film *Death of a Gandy Dancer* (SCA, 1977) shows the special fun of hearing true stories of a grandfather's younger days. After the children have been exposed to different ways the generations interact in these stories, they can talk about their own intergenerational relationships. Ask children: What do they know today because someone taught it to them? What do they like to do with their parents, with grandparents, or with other older adults? Do they help around the house or at their grandparents'? Have children demonstrate some skill or activity they have learned and ask who taught them it.

- Children can role play an older person and young child interacting. The child playing the older person acts out teaching the one in the child role a task or skill. Have the young child act out a way she might show her appreciation to the older person. Ask children if younger people ever teach older people. What and how? When do people stop learning and teaching?

- Give children a set of activities that require the help of an older person: for example, a crossword puzzle with questions about historical events and famous people from earlier times, or learning to do the twist or the waltz and identifying the music on tape. Children could ask classroom volunteers for help, or take the activities home to complete with parents, grandparents, or older friends and neighbors. Older volunteers can help you come up with questions or activities; they may think of people whom the children might not know and whom you might not think of, such as radio characters, comedy teams, or inventors. They'll probably think of some old-time activities you would never dream of, as well.

Elders can share cherished skills with children, linking the generations in pleasure.

OBJECTIVE: *To enable children to identify the contributions older people make.*

- Read the African tale *Mother Crocodile* (Guy, 1981) . In this story, little crocodiles find that stories passed down from generation to generation give them lifesaving information; "old talk" may sound crazy, but elders contribute in important ways as they share their knowledge. In addition, show a film about intergenerational programs such as *Close Harmony* (SCA, 1981). What do the children feel the older volunteers in their classroom have contributed to their experience? Make a list of contributions, and ask children to plan a special appreciation for these volunteers. Let them use their creative ideas to plan a party or show, or to make a videotape for the volunteers.

- Have speakers from service organizations with elderly members come to talk about the work they do in the community.

- Research the life of an older person in the school or community. What contributions did this person make to the community?

- Give the children a variety of construction materials — scrap papers, empty boxes, wires, ribbons, plastic scraps, tape, staples, and glue — and ask them to invent something, or change something already invented.

- Survey several local companies for information on the type of work they do, the workers' average age, and the average age of retirement. Parents can also help children understand the composition of the work force by listing jobs done in their offices and approximate ages of the workers. The children can examine the data to see whether the type of work might influence the age of the workers. Further, children can keep a diary or log of the different occupations they see when they are out of school on field trips, vacations, and weekends, or at dental or medical appointments. Have children indicate which of these were or could have been performed by elderly people.

- Make a list of places children go regularly. Ask them to observe if there are older people at these places. Give them a week to find out what the older people are doing. Make sure that not everyone will be observing people in the same place by assigning some children to the library, some to the mall, some to the neighborhood, and so on. How are the activities of the older people different from those of the younger people? How are the activities the same? Were some of the people doing the same things that the children were doing? Were they surprised at some of the activities they observed?

To enable children to feel positive about their own aging and the elderly.

OBJECTIVE: *To develop knowledge of the continuity of life and of past, present, and future.*

- Have the children list on a chart a number of objects and activities with which they are familiar (see Figure on page 30). Ask them to interview their parents, grandparents, or older neighbors to find out what these things were like when they were six, seven, or eight years old. After making the charts, children can play "Who Am I?" A child reads one list from her chart. The class then tries to guess whether the child is reading about herself, her mother, or her grandmother. What things are the same and what are different? Which items gave it away or stumped them? The children could speculate about how and why these things might differ in the future. How will they be the same persons in the future and how will they be different? The discussion could lead to the children painting what life will be like in the future, or writing a creative story.

- Read *Storm in the Night* (Stoltz, 1988), in which a boy has a hard time imagining that his grandfather was once a child. Yet his grandfather says that he talked and looked like the boy when he was young. Then his grandfather tells a story of being afraid of a storm in the night, and the boy sees that his grandfather really may have been like him after all. After reading the story, ask the children if their parents or grandparents were ever afraid of anything. Can they imagine the adults they know as children? Can they imagine themselves as adults? Ask children to draw a picture of how they will look at ages 15, 45, and 70 or to write a story about what they will do when they are grown up.

- Ask children to think about some of the most important events of their life and list these with their age and the approximate date of the event. Then they can speculate about what other important events may occur in the future. Children can make their own timelines beginning with their birth and showing these important events that have already occurred (entering school, riding a bike, moving, etc.) and those they expect or hope will occur (graduating from high school or college, getting married, starting work, retiring, making a great invention, or living on the moon).

- Children can dictate or write stories about their life in school. Ask them to write about the things they learned in first grade, are currently learning, and plan to learn in the future.

Figure: Being seven — now and then

	When I Was Seven	When My Mother Was Seven	When My Grandmother Was Seven
Food			
Clothing			
Shopping			
Games			
Play			
School			
Neighborhood			
Television			
Travel			

OBJECTIVE: *To extend children's number concepts and concepts of age/time relationships.*

- Ask children to solve mathematics problems such as: How old will you be in three years? How old will your mother be in four years? If you are seven and your brother is two, how much older are you and how much younger is he? Mary is seven, Lisa 11 — who is older and by how much?

- Have children make booklets about their extended family with an illustration and story about each member. Ask several children to write the oldest person's age on the board and the youngest person's age under it. Then as a class find the difference in ages. Whose family has the largest difference in ages? Does anyone in the class think his family has a larger gap in ages? Continue to get class volunteers to set up problems on the board until the largest gap is found.

- Children will be interested in ages of everything — from pets to houses. Have them find out the ages of five things their family has, and compile a class list of "Ages of Things." Talk about how some things last longer than others. What are the oldest things the families have? What are the newest or youngest things?

Evaluating the curriculum _____

But does it work? Is the curriculum effective in fostering children's knowledge of age and in promoting positive attitudes toward maturing and toward the elderly? Are you achieving the goals? Evaluation, a necessary part of all curriculum planning, not only enables you to judge the effectiveness of the curriculum and achievement of goals, but also gives you the information needed to improve the curriculum. Evaluation shows you which teaching techniques are effective, which activities foster children's understanding, and which areas need improvement.

Observing children

Most evaluation is informal and takes place all of the time. As you observe children playing, talking with one another about some experience or story, or interacting with the elderly, you naturally reflect on the classroom activities and experiences. Listening to Alberto and Sue playing house, you hear Sue say, "I'm making pancakes with maple syrup for Grandpa — it's his favorite." Alberto responds, "Pancakes are my favorite too." You recognize that the children are using ideas from the previous week's discussion about foods both young and old people enjoy.

Informal, unobtrusive observations of children yield a great deal of information about a program's effectiveness; however, as a means of evaluation, they require an understanding of children, knowledge of curriculum content, and skill. When teachers observe children in the classroom, they must be objective and focus only on actual behaviors. Keep in mind these guidelines:

- Describe the behavior rather than give interpretations of it.
- Focus observations on all aspects of children's developing concepts and attitudes of age and the elderly.
- Describe the surrounding environment and what happened prior to and after the recorded incident.
- Observe children at different times of the day in different situations and settings.
- Focus the intent of the observations by referring back to the curriculum goals.

One teacher observing children during outdoor play recorded, "The children have adjusted well to the changes that come with age." She backed up this subjective statement with a story of the children asking an elderly volunteer to play with them in the sandbox. When the volunteer explained that she could not sit down in the sandbox, the children brought out a chair from the classroom so that she could sit near them as they played.

For more formal observations, compile a check list from the curriculum goals and note children's progress in achieving them. In addition, you might interview children, asking them how they will feel when they are old, what they know about old people, and what they do with old people.

Using standardized instruments

The problems with using standardized evaluation instruments are that they consume both children's and teacher's time and are not sensitive to context. They are useful in comparing programs, however. See Appendix B for a number of these tests.

The *Children's Attitudes Toward the Elderly* test (Seefeldt, Jantz, Galper, & Serock, 1976) combines structured interviews with standardized methods. The first section consists of open ended questions that elicit children's feelings about growing old and about the elderly. Asking the children these questions before and after the curriculum experience will illustrate the curriculum's effectiveness. In the second

"I'm making pancakes with maple syrup for grandpa — it's his favorite." Informal and unobtrusive observations of children yield a great deal of information about a program's effectiveness in fostering children's knowledge of age and in promoting positive attitudes toward the elderly.

section of the test, the teacher reads bipolar adjectives for the concepts of old and young and asks the children to respond to them, either orally or in writing. The final part consists of pictures of a man at four ages, 20, 40, 60, and 80. Children tell which man is the youngest and which is the oldest and then put the four pictures in chronological order. They also say which man they would prefer to be with and what they would do with the youngest and oldest man pictured.

PART 2

Intergenerational Programs That Support Curriculum

Through successful intergenerational programs, children and older people interact with one another, reestablishing the caring relationships Margaret Mead (1970) believed vital for the continuity of all cultures. Children interacting with a number of older people find that they give up some of their stereotypical thinking of aging and the elderly. Having daily contact with them tends to prevent children thinking of the old as tired and sick, for they will see that being old does not preclude living a life of fulfillment and joy. They will come to see older people as individuals with diverse characteristics, strengths, and weaknesses. Elders report that they enjoy being with children and that children do make good friends for older people. Furthermore, as a group, elders have a great deal of knowledge about children's growth and development and of effective methods of working with children.

Many current intergenerational programs take place in infant day care centers or with children under the age of three. Elder volunteers care for babies, holding, rocking, and cuddling them, and interact with toddlers. Some of these programs are identified in Appendix B. This manual, however, focuses on programs serving children from ages three to eight.

Criteria for good intergenerational programs _____

Regardless of type of program, the involvement of the elderly with children must have integrity. To promote caring between the generations and to enable children to think more positively about their own aging and the elderly, contact between old and young must be intimate, pleasurable, and rewarding for both groups. The time spent together should be meaningful, making use of the children's interests and the elders' skills and talents, with both young and old involved in setting goals and participating in important activities.

There is very real danger that newly created intergenerational programs will perpetuate negative stereotypes that the elderly are childish. If the elderly are treated like children, that's the message children will get. If children are to develop positive attitudes toward the old and their own aging, contact in the schools must protect elders' prestige. Instead of asking elders to take on the role of children, to complete silly tasks like cutting out dozens of bunnies, or to dress in funny hats, make sure that the elderly are given meaningful tasks. Asking older people to share skills, relate stories of their past, play with children, and interact with them in other meaningful ways can promote feelings of oneness with children and foster positive images of aging.

Elders can help determine program activities. They will be more committed to a program that really makes use of their experience and skills and allows them to share these experiences in their own way. The program will also be enriched because the children will see for themselves that elders are a unique group of individuals, with individual talents, interests, and abilities that are of value to children, schools, and society.

Frustration on the part of elders, children, teachers, and other school personnel is minimized when someone is clearly in charge of the program and everyone understands the volunteers' role. Careful plans for the elders' time, training, supervision, and recognition must be made.

Beginning a program _____

Setting goals

Before beginning an intergenerational program, take some time to dream, as dreaming is a form of goal setting. Then establish specific goals for the total program, the children, and the elders.

Some sample goals for the total program may be:

- to increase frequency of contact between generations
- to foster positive attitudes between generations
- to provide additional services for children with special needs
- to meet older people's needs for growth and development
- to foster a sense of continuity of life for both old and young

Goals can specifically relate to the program's goals. Two examples of goals for children's growth come from the Teaching-Learning Communities project. One goal was that when working with an elder volunteer, children would complete more craft projects. Another goal was that children would maintain materials and supplies in art centers with the volunteers' assistance. Other goals might be that children will:

- appreciate relating with older people
- develop an understanding of the aging process
- increase positive attitudes toward their own aging and the elderly
- improve in specific academic skills
- receive support from an older person
- learn new skills

Goals set by and for the elderly volunteers might include:

- sharing knowledge and skills with children
- increasing their circle of friends
- improving physical and mental health
- developing an increased sense of worth and importance
- feeling the love of children
- helping the school community

Different programs will have different goals. Think specifically about what results you want and how you would know whether or not the program had been successful. What behaviors would let you know that the goals had been achieved? You could read about other programs, or contact people who have successfully implemented intergenerational programs (see Appendix B).

Time spent together should be meaningful, making use of the children's interests and the elders' skills and talents.

Role of the coordinator

Successful intergenerational programs are planned. One step in planning is to designate someone in the school to have full responsibility for the volunteer project's overall direction and supervision. It may not always be possible to hire another staff member, but someone must be in charge. This person will do most of the planning and develop the program. The coordinator of volunteers will:

- plan the program's goals
- plan the budget and obtain outside funding
- arrange space within the building for the volunteers
- obtain or develop materials to be used as program resources
- plan and schedule the volunteers' times
- recruit, orient, and train volunteers
- prepare the staff and children to work with the older person
- supervise the total program
- be available for the volunteers to talk to, keeping an open line of communication
- make plans for recognition for the volunteers
- evaluate the total program

It's not that this person does these things alone, without involving the other staff, children, parents, and especially the older people, but that she or he coordinates the entire planning process and program.

Liability insurance is a must when involving the elderly in any program. Coordinators are responsible for checking the school's insurance plan to make certain the older volunteers are covered. Furthermore, all who come in contact with children may need a health check; most states require a TB check at the minimum. The coordinator must determine the regulations and arrange for these to be met.

Most programs involving older people find that they need to arrange for transportation for the volunteers, or at least reimburse some of their transportation costs. You will also want to arrange for the volunteers to eat lunch at the school and to include them in snack times with the children. The older people may wish to eat with the children, or as a separate group.

Intergenerational programs are not without cost. In addition to insurance, transportation, and meals, you may need supplies for orientation and training, and those to use with the children. The coordinator should look into obtaining outside funding through foundations or federal grants. Some agency in the community might offer a grant, or perhaps your own board of directors could budget for the program.

Preparing teachers

All staff who work directly with elders need to be involved in planning. If staff are not aware of the project's goals, or of the preparation for the elders, they may see the older person as just one more thing they have to worry about. Often, teachers of young children have little experience supervising or giving directions to others, especially when the other people are more experienced and older than they.

It is beneficial for teachers to understand that one developmental aspect of aging is integrating one's life experiences. The older person is naturally reviewing his life and evaluating its meaning (Erikson, Erikson, & Kivnick, 1986). Sharing with children the skills and knowledge he has acquired over a lifetime can help an older person recognize the meaningfulness of his life's experiences. Older people volunteer when it is meaningful and self-fulfilling for them to do so (Chambré, 1987). Therefore, it makes sense to find ways for older volunteers to share their knowledge and skills in the classroom.

Teachers also need to develop patience and understanding in working with the elderly, just as they are patient with children and let them learn at their own pace. Any volunteer will be overwhelmed by a teacher who too quickly gives instructions without elaborating. If, however, you take the time to make sure you are understood and the volunteers are confident, you will be rewarded. Elders are not volunteering simply to work for the teacher. Each volunteer must have a special place in the program that makes her experience meaningful.

Some training or preparation in how to supervise the volunteers, work with them, give assignments, and plan for their activity is useful for teachers. They should also think about how they will prepare for the elder and set their own goals for the volunteer for this current group of children or for an individual child.

Preparing children

Children also need time to adjust their thinking. Young children should be told in advance that someone else will be in their group, and they need time to prepare for this person. Sometimes real guidance may be necessary. Ask the children to think of ways to make the elder feel welcome: "How will we let Ms. Smith know our names?" "Who will show her where to put her coat?" "How will we get ready for lunch?" One teacher asked the children to take turns being the greeter. Together they decided on the greeter's responsibilities. There was always a waiting list for this role. Telling the children something of the older person's special talents, interests, or background may help

Facts about the elderly

Approximately one out of every four Americans is over 50 years of age, and the proportion is growing. By 2030, it is estimated that one in three Americans will be over 50.

Older people no more fit a stereotype than members of other arbitrary groupings of people. The only blanket assertion that applies to all senior citizens is that they have lived longer. They come from every stratum of society, are active in their communities, and have friends, families, and lovers. Older people are individuals and showing them as such can add variety and depth to communications between young and old.

Senior citizens represent every economic level: affluent, middle class, and poor. Eighty-eight percent of those age 65 and older have adequate incomes. Nonetheless, poverty is a fact of life for all too many elderly people, particularly women and minorities. Approximately 12% of people age 50 and above have incomes below the poverty line and 13% are considered near poor.

Most elderly people are self-sufficient. In 1983, 67% lived independently — alone, with family members, or with nonrelatives. About 18% have other living arrangements, such as retirement communities or villages. Nursing homes are not an inevitable or even likely result of growing old. Only 5% of Americans age 65 and above live in nursing homes at any one time.

About 76% of men and 46% of women over 50 live with their spouses. Seven percent of older men and 18% of older women live with other relatives or nonrelated people. Love and sexuality are a part of aging. Meaningful personal relationships are as important in the later years as they are in youth.

Elders are concerned about their communities and take action. In the 1980 presidential election, 67.7% of those 50 years and over voted. Twenty-eight percent of people older than 50 devote time to volunteer work in the community.

Age alone is not an adequate explanation for elderly people's attitudes and values; their source lies in the accumulation of past experiences and societal factors.

Many of today's older generation were born just after the turn of the century, and their experiences have been substantially different from those of succeeding generations. When they were attending school, for example, norms of educational attainment were much lower than they are today. Similarly, this generation was trained for occupations and taught skills that in some cases have become obsolete. The technological changes this group has witnessed are phenomenal — many elders were born before the airplane and automobile were in widespread use.

Note: Based on *Truth About Aging,* 1986, Washington, DC: American Association for Retired Persons.

the children to establish relationships with the person. Read books such as *Song and Dance Man* (Ackerman, 1988) to the children before the person comes.

Children need to be informed of and to plan for any physical disability the older person may have. For instance, if the elder uses a cane or some other type of assistance, the children should understand why the person needs it as well as how they are to act and help. Discussions enable children to sort out their own feelings about aging and the elderly before the volunteer comes to the class. This preparation will enable the children to feel secure and open to the new experiences they will have.

Recruiting the elderly

A number of organizations and associations that recruit and train senior citizens to work with children are listed in Appendix B. If one of these associations is not present in your community, there are other effective ways of recruiting volunteers. One way is by word of mouth. As children and their parents register for the program, explain the idea of intergenerational contact as a part of the child care, nursery school, preschool, or primary program. Parents may know of an older person —a friend, relative, or neighbor—who would be eager to volunteer.

Sometimes volunteers are not the usual "joiners" but people identified as special by someone who knows them. When you hear of a person with an especially interesting hobby or life experience, it can be very worthwhile to actively recruit the individual. One elderly man was asked to come to the school as a special speaker. This initial contact grew into a 20-hour-a-week commitment for him. Many elderly people do not see themselves in a volunteer role until they understand that they have something unique to offer.

Just talking about the program to others at social gatherings, or in the neighborhood, leads to finding people interested in working with young children. Some programs develop a slide-tape recruitment presentation to show to religious groups or civic organizations. An attractive brochure concisely describing the intergenerational program's goals is useful for distribution to associations within the community, retirement homes, or places of worship. The existence of a volunteer program appeals to the local media; children and elders together are a fine human interest story.

Preparing children is an important step in program development.

Establishing the program

Together, the staff, coordinator, and volunteers decide on the role the elders will take. A review of the policies of the child care program or school is necessary. In some school districts no one but the teacher may be responsible for anything considered academic in nature. Other programs stipulate that the staff must be present at all times and never leave a room when a volunteer is working with children.

Once policies are understood, the types of things volunteers will do with children can be determined. Any activity or experience is possible. Flexibility and creativity are important to match the skills of the elders and the needs of the children, teacher, and school. Some elders will tutor children in school work; others may help children with special needs. Some may teach skills, crafts, or games; others may be available just to talk with children. The activity must be of interest to the older person and the children.

A check list of skills, hobbies, and activities will facilitate interviews with potential volunteers. It is important to identify what each volunteer's strengths are. Their answers to questions like the following help the coordinator get to know them.

- What kind of work have you done?
- What is your favorite pastime?
- Which age group do you like to work with?
- Do you have any special hobbies?

Some volunteers may not wish to work directly with children. They may decide that support services are better suited to their interests and skills. They could do clerical tasks, prepare materials, or help with other aspects of the program. If a senior citizen wishes to work "behind the scenes," it is still important for someone to introduce her or him to the children. Then children will know and recognize that older people do care about them and work to help them.

Orientation and training _____

Cultivating commitment

Volunteering can be a sometime thing if commitment is not established. If older people do not feel bound to the program and do not know their work is crucial, it's easy for them to drop out, or to come only when they have nothing better to do. Thus, the first stage in orientation and training is to establish the importance of the volunteer's role and to build commitment to the program.

Establish a feeling of membership by involving the new volunteer with a group, perhaps of other volunteers or of the staff. In a group, volunteers experience the friendship, warmth, and commitment of others and begin to see themselves as part of a team.

Have the principal or administrator welcome the group to the program. The school is happy to have a diverse group, and if the principal acknowledges the diversity among the volunteers and the jobs they will do, individual volunteers will see that their contributions are unique and important. In addition, providing volunteers with information about the program will communicate the importance of their presence. Inform them of program goals, how the program works, and some of its successes, and relate anecdotes about children.

It may also be possible to cultivate commitment by meeting some other needs the older person has. Some elders may feel the need for social activities and friendships, others help in obtaining social services or health care. In one school, the older volunteers got together and arranged for a police officer to teach them techniques of self-defense. Another child care center was able to set up a free trip to the symphony.

Then, too, commitment comes when the elders' wishes are respected. Elders say they want to have some control over their contact with children. Certainly they can decide which age group they work with, whether they work with an individual child or a group, and for how long and on which days they come to the center or school.

Building security

Insecurity is not unusual when first beginning a new job or entering a new group. One part of orientation and training should be designed to build a sense of security. Just talking with the person is helpful. Describe the nature of the program to the volunteer, and have the children and the elder discuss their skills, interests, or concerns.

Explain their role to the volunteers as clearly as you can. Give them a tour of the building to observe the child care program. As you take the volunteers around, introducing them to the faculty and children, point out how children are learning and the special techniques teachers use as they work with individual children or small groups. Be sure to establish a routine for the volunteers to follow upon arrival. They will want to know where to check in for the day, whom they should contact with any problems, where they will go for lunch, and when the transportation home will leave.

It is very important to have some handouts or a volunteer booklet for elders to refer to and to make sure their questions are answered. Some volunteers may wish to do additional reading about children and learning or about other intergenerational programs. Having books and articles available to check out allows volunteers to obtain this information easily.

Make sure that the volunteers experience success at the start. Plan for them to work with one child or a small group, or do something that will be immediately gratifying. You might ask them to bring in an object that will interest the children. One elder who collected fossils brought a huge fossilized shark's tooth. Another brought flowers from her garden along with seeds for the children to plant in individual cups. If the person plays the piano, knits, or is a good storyteller, for example, then that's what she should do on her first visit.

Training volunteers

"Do those wrinkles hurt you a lot?" asks a curious four-year-old of an older volunteer, who gasps at the perceived rudeness of the question. Older people who understand something about children's curiosity will not misinterpret such a question. Others not as familiar with children or the methods of the center or school may need more preparation.

Observing is a good way to become familiar with children. Perhaps a person more familiar with children could be paired with another whose background does not include contact with children. Ask an experienced and an inexperienced volunteer to observe together and compare observations informally.

Teachers should also be prepared to explain their methods and actions. One elder was horrified to see a child sitting alone at a table crying loudly but ignored by the teacher, who was working with another child. As he went to comfort the crying child, the teacher explained, "It's OK. I know you must think I'm cruel, but Ron will stop crying in a moment. He is learning to gain control and to ask, instead of scream, for what he wants." Teachers may casually but carefully tell how they set limits for children. A teacher, having asked child to put a toy down before climbing on the monkey bars, mentioned to the volunteer, "I always try to tell the children what I want them to do instead of what not to do — that way they do it because they know what I want."

Although elders will best come to understand their role through on-the-job training, in many instances training is easiest in a group. Invite volunteers to take part in a regularly scheduled staff meeting, or in special meetings to deal with topics such as discipline. In a group, the volunteers can discuss their experiences, solve problems, share their expertise, watch films and filmstrips, and listen to speakers. As

To ensure their successful interactions with children, volunteers should undergo training.

legislation has changed children's programs dramatically (for instance, the laws guaranteeing the rights of handicapped children and their families to equal educational opportunity, and child abuse and neglect laws), consider holding a meeting to explore current legislation and determine how the volunteers can assume a role in fulfilling its intent. You might even recruit elders for the sole purpose of working with children who have special needs. Discuss in groups other concerns facing people who work with children today, such as the dangers of stereotyping on the basis of sex, race, and age; the importance of using language free from sex-role stereotypes; the rights of children and their families to confidentiality; and the use and abuse of standardized tests.

As mentioned, the best training is on the job — that is, as long as there is a supervisor, coordinator, or teacher in charge who is willing and able to give feedback. A good training technique, feedback lets volunteers know how effective they are as they work directly with children. You can comment on the effectiveness of different strategies. For example, you might point out how interested the children were when the volunteer showed the pictures as she told the story, or the specific skills a child has gained by being with her.

Feedback also opens up lines of communication among volunteers, teachers, and administrators. Specific feedback helps the elders know that the children and teachers are really interested in them and appreciate their efforts. The coordinator can point out ways the elder makes a unique contribution to the growth of a child or the program.

Encourage volunteers to interact and compare experiences. A room in the building and time for volunteers to meet and share their expertise is another forum for feedback. This space can be as informal as a reserved lunchroom table, or as formal as separate volunteers' room.

Recognizing volunteers

Volunteering to work with children is intrinsically rewarding. When elders see the joy children receive from their presence and recognize their contribution to cementing relations between generations, few outside rewards are necessary. Yet, no matter how fulfilling his role is, or how important the volunteer perceives his tasks, outside acknowledgment is important. Receiving recognition along with supervision and increased responsibility has been linked with the continuing satisfaction and participation of the elderly in volunteer programs (Chambré, 1987).

The idea of budgeting for some type of monetary compensation for the volunteers should be considered. It seems important in our society for people to receive remuneration for their work. If a job is really important, people receive pay. But money isn't always enough. Volunteers must received recognition from their peers, their colleagues, and the public.

Newspaper and media coverage provides one form of recognition. Call the local newspaper and explain the program and the work of the volunteer. Arrange a photo session, perhaps cutting pumpkins for Halloween, or story time with the elder reading to children on his lap.

Another idea is to give the elder a framed certificate of appreciation from the school or program with her name on it. Think about individualizing this certificate of appreciation. Some examples:

- a memento built of small toy alphabet blocks spelling out the volunteer's name and "thank you" to one woman who especially enjoyed children's block buildings
- an experience chart with each child dictating something about the volunteer and either drawing a picture or writing her or his name on the chart, which the teacher then recopied in a more manageable size and framed
- a booklet with a dictated or written thank you from each child
- a big book written around the refrain "We love you, Ms. Smith," with pages describing all of the things Ms. Smith did with the children
- a framed photograph of all the children gathered on a jungle gym for the volunteer who designed and supervised the building of a new playyard

An end-of-the-year awards lunch, banquet, or meeting is usually well attended and received. The intergenerational program director, city council members, and other important people from the community, perhaps even the mayor, should be invited to attend. The program director, the mayor, or the children can present the volunteers with certificates of apprecitaion or framed awards.

Rewards and recognition, like training, are continual, and they do not always need to be formal. A thank you at the end of the day by the teacher, a hug from a child, or recognition of a special task completed successfully will make the volunteer feel appreciated.

Volunteers appreciate knowing they are valued.

Evaluating the program _____

Evaluation contributes to all aspects of maintaining an intergenerational program. Decide early in the project what types of evaluation you will use; they will depend on the goals and objectives you selected for the program. There are many ways to determine how effective the project has been, whether or not the goals have been achieved, and which areas need improvement. Using more than one evaluation method will give you a more complete picture.

If the objective is to increase the amount of individualized attention the children receive, for example, volunteers or the teacher could document the amount of time an adult spent with each child before and during the intergenerational program. Evaluation is more than looking at numbers, however. You also want to know if this added attention is satisfying and beneficial to all. Do the volunteers find their tasks boring or fulfilling? Do the teachers find they need to give so much assistance to the volunteers that it is not worth the effort? Which children seem to benefit the most from the additional attention? Some program directors ask these kinds of questions throughout the year at weekly or monthly conferences with staff and volunteers. This type of evaluation, called *formative,* helps the director shape and improve the program.

For more formal answers, administer questionnaires before, midway through, and at the end of the program. Use the differences in individuals' responses over time to sum up how effective the project has been. This is called *summative* evaluation.

Another method is to distribute a questionnaire only at the end of the program. For example, one program focused on teacher satisfaction, and for the evaluation the director developed and administered a teacher questionnaire. Teachers listed numerous benefits of having volunteers work with them. They also said their feelings about their own aging and the elderly were more positive as a result of their interaction with the volunteers. Another program had the priority of having as many elder volunteers as possible involved. The director tallied the number of elders involved with the children and the school and distributed a questionnaire querying volunteer satisfaction. Although high numbers of people were involved, satisfaction was low. There was high turnover, and the volunteers said it was not worth their time because they did not have enough training or understanding of what their role was in the project to feel successful.

You might administer a standardized instrument, as described in Part One, as an element in your evaluation process. For example, if one of the project's goals is to improve children's attitudes toward their own aging and the elderly, you could give the *Children's Attitudes Toward the Elderly* test (Seefeldt, Jantz, Galper, & Serock, 1976) before and after the program to determine attitude change.

In addition, observe children and elders interacting and keep a record of these interactions. Look for instances of elders and children hugging, talking together, and sharing one another's joys, interests, and love. Try to record what children and elders say as well as how they act toward one another. These observation records, when combined with standardized test results, yield powerful information on the program's effectiveness.

Because evaluation is self-reflective, and therefore difficult, you might consider having an uninvolved, objective party conduct the evaluations. Local universities and colleges may be interested in the program and willing to do some observing and consulting for you, or an advisory board could be in charge of assessing the program.

Evaluation results give the program coordinator information to pass on during volunteer recognition and recruitment. When public support is needed to fund the program, the documented successes and needs can be publicized. In planning training and supervision, the findings will serve as a guide. In short, evaluation contributes to all aspects of maintaining a high quality, successful intergenerational program.

APPENDIX
A
Curriculum Materials

Stereotypes abound! Even though the elderly are a diverse group of people, too often there is the tendency to think of them as helpless, bored, or senile. Think of the stereotypes of the little old lady rocking on the porch knitting all day while nearby her unkempt, ornery husband dozes, or of the helpless old woman who needs a boy scout to help her cross the street and the senile old man who cannot remember his way home. Children learn these stereotypes in the classroom, at home, or in the community. Children's attitudes toward aging and older people are influenced by real-life models as well as images and terms in the media and the school's instructional materials. Nuessel (1989) points out that ageism is present in the adjectives and nouns used to describe older people. He found that in the American vocabulary older people are often referred to as "toothless," "crotchety," and "witless," or labeled as fools, grumps, codgers, and coots.

When choosing materials for children, we need to be aware of ageism and stereotypes. Look for materials that portray the elderly in realistic, nonstereotypic ways. Evaluate the materials' language, content, and message, as well as their appropriateness for young children. How many times are the elderly portrayed in the materials children use? When elderly are present, are they shown taking the initiative, solving problems, earning money, and gaining recognition? Are they portrayed active or passive? Fearful or brave? Helpless or helpful? Do they participate in a wide range of activities? How many different roles do the characters have?

Yes, it is true: Some old people do become ill, are senile, or cannot take care of themselves. There again, most older people do work, have hobbies, and can tell the most fascinating stories. The idea here is that the old are a diverse population, more different than alike. The materials used in the classroom should reflect the diversity of older people and the richness of intergenerational relationships. Not all books, filmstrips, and videotapes need to depict the old in active, strong roles. What's important is that children see a balance of depictions. Children enjoy *Grandfather and I* (Buckley, 1965), in which the grandfather and grandchild have all the time in the world. Grandfather is slow and does not mind taking time to look around at insects and trains. This is a lovely, sweet story of togetherness. Yet the book has been criticized as presenting a stereotypical image of the old as slow, inactive, and unable to do much but walk. On the other hand, *Song and Dance Man* (Ackerman, 1988) shows a grandfather doing his vaudeville routine for his grandchildren. Together, these books, and others in the following lists, provide children with a balanced, realistic portrayal of the elderly.

When you do find stereotypical images, challenge them. You might ask the class, "Do you remember Ms. Smith? What do you think she would have done?" "Do you think all old people are as silly as this man in the story?" "Is every old person so helpless?"

In discussing bibliotherapy, the use of literature in helping children deal with emotions, Jalongo (1983) explains that teachers who hope to address feelings, attitudes, beliefs, and values with this therapy should:

- be thoroughly familiar with the book content;
- prepare to introduce the story by pointing out the book's relevance to everyday life;
- prepare specific questions to use throughout the story; and
- summarize the story's meaning and the children's emotional responses.

The discussion questions and other activities for the books and media suggested in Part One of this manual are meant to stimulate your thoughts on how to use the materials. Jalongo (1983) suggests that books and media will not substitute for your own preparation and understanding of the group of children you have, but they can stimulate your own ideas.

Books and films are listed here by curriculum objectives and can be used with our curriculum suggestions, or without. We also list several guides and bibliographies for choosing children's literature, followed by materials to assist in planning curriculum activities.

The annotations will help you decide which books will interest your class. Try using some books in groups, having volunteers read some to individuals, and making others available for children to read or look at on their own. Books listed here are suitable for preschoolers, kindergartners, and primary grade children unless otherwise noted. Often, you can use long or complex books with younger children by condensing them, by focusing on the illustrations to tell the story, and by asking lots of questions. Be especially sure to acquaint yourself with the characters and to have appropriate discussion questions for stereotypical and sensitive materials.

You should also preview the films and videos and pick out sections your children will find interesting. Films containing interviews with a variety of people can easily be broken up for viewing over several class periods. Ask children questions ahead of time and during the showing to help them focus on the film and relate it to their experiences at home and at school.

Enabling children to feel positive about their own aging

These materials are good for beginning to explore children's attitudes toward aging. They address attitudes by showing children struggling with what it means to grow up, challenging the stereotypes of aging, depicting children changing their minds about older people once they get to know them, and introducing some positive intergenerational relationships.

Children's books

Berenstain, J., & Berenstain, S. (1986). *The Berenstain Bears and the week at Grandma's.* New York: Random House.

The cubs learn a lot about their grandparents during a week's stay. After some doubts about the visit, they find their grandparents to be fun, interesting, and lovable. They learn from their grandparents and appreciate how wise they are.

Blos, J. (1987). *Old Henry.* New York: William Morrow.

When an older person moves into a run-down house, his neighbors think he is going to fix it up. Instead he is busy with his reading, birds, painting, and cooking. The neighbors, young and old, learn that Henry is actually a very interesting person who should be appreciated for who he is instead of changed to what they think he should be.

Cosgrove, S. (1981). *Grampa-Lop.* Los Angeles: Price/Stern/Sloan. Story cassette also available.

The young rabbits love Grampa-Lop's stories, but the older rabbits think he is silly. Finally, the children make the other adults realize the value of Grampa-Lop's stories. Use of animals makes the story especially appealing to young children.

Griffith, H. (1987). *Granddaddy's place.* New York: Greenwillow.

This book for primary grade children depicts a city girl visiting her grandfather in the country, which seems to her full of mean and ugly things. She quickly picks up on her granddaddy's humor and soon is imitating his tall tales. She learns to love him and his lifestyle.

Guy, R. (1981). *Mother crocodile.* (Translated and adapted from Birago Diop's story "Maman-Caiman"). New York: Delacorte.

An African tale for kindergartners through third graders relates the story of little crocodiles who think "old talk is crazy." When one of these stories saves their lives, they gain respect for the elderly and the stories passed down from generation to generation.

Hurd, E. (1982). *I dance in my red pajamas.* New York: Harper & Row.

Jenny's grandparents are not as "old" as her parents seem to think. They are active and exciting to be with. This story of a child visiting her grandparents challenges stereotypes. Not only does Jenny find older people to be active, she discovers that they dance romantically, too.

Hutchins, P. (1971). *Titch.* New York: Macmillan.

Titch always feels small and unimportant next to his siblings; everything he has is smaller than what they have. When he and his brother and sister each plant a seed, his is again the smallest. As time goes on, however, the seed grows so big that it is even taller than his big sister and brother. A good book for preschoolers.

Hutchins, P. (1983). *You'll soon grow into them.* New York: Greenwillow.

A predictable book for preschoolers about growing. Titch grows out of his clothes and gets hand-me-downs that are too large. Finally, when he has a new baby brother, he can pass his clothes on

and tell the baby what everyone has been telling him, "You'll soon grow into them."

Krauss, R. (1947). *The growing story.* New York: Harper & Brothers.

Another book appropriate for preschoolers about a child who discovers that he is growing up because his clothes no longer fit.

Lasker, J. (1982). *The do-something day.* New York: Viking.

This book, set in New York City in the 1950s, is full of older people with different ethnic backgrounds working in their shops. These are Bernie's friends, who find jobs for him when he wants to help but his family is too busy to give him something to do. Some stereotypes are present.

McPhail, D. (1980). *Pig Pig grows up.* New York: Dutton.

Pig Pig wants to be a baby forever and refuses to grow up. Preschoolers and kindergartners will enjoy the silliness of seeing a grown pig in baby clothes. Although the children can see how silly he is, Pig Pig does not act his age until he discovers he can help others.

Stevenson, J. (1977). *Could be worse.* New York: Greenwillow.

When the children complain about how boring Grandfather is, he tells a fantastic adventure story. Grandfather is really not so boring after all. Like many older adults, he is a great storyteller. Humorous to elementary school children.

Zolotow, C. (1984). *I know a lady.* New York: Greenwillow.

Every season brings new treats for the children in this old lady's neighborhood. The child narrator is curious about the woman and wonders if someone gave her treats when she was a child. A simple story written in an entrancing way.

Films

Forever young. (1981). Opus Films, 63 E. 82nd St., New York, NY 10028. 60 mins. Color. 16mm

Aging is viewed as a positive thing. The film interviews 26 older people with a variety of interests and occupations. Included are skydivers, artists, and farmers.

Free to be . . . you and me. (1974). New York: McGraw-Hill. 42 min. Color. 16mm. Also available on videocassette.

The film shows a variety of people, both young and old, and focuses on the diversity among all people and the right to be yourself.

The joy of communication. (1975). Dana Productions, 6249 Babcock Ave., North Hollywood, CA 91606. 18 min. Color. 16mm

With music and pictures, this film shows communication between people of all ages. Children can see that older people enjoy different kinds of interaction with younger people. Sometimes the younger people care for the elderly, and sometimes the elderly help the younger people.

The shopping bag lady. (1975). Learning Corporation of America, 108 Wilmot Rd., Deerfield, IL 60015. 22 min. Color. 16mm

A 14-year-old girl changes her attitude toward the elderly when she finds that a shopping bag lady carries old photos with her. She realizes that old people have feelings and can be interesting, too.

Providing children with accurate information and knowledge about the elderly _____

These materials give children an understanding that the elderly are a diverse group of people with emotions and experiences similar to their own. These materials can help children comprehend their own growing/aging and the passage of time. Many introduce the relationships of parents and grandparents.

Children's books

Ackerman, K. (1988). *Song and dance man.* New York: Knopf.

Grandfather pulls out his tap shoes and bowler hat from an old trunk in the attic. He proceeds to amaze and excite his grandchildren by performing his vaudeville act. The story not only depicts a very active grandfather playing with his grandchildren, it also shows that he has saved things that are important to him and that he once lived a different life. Caldecott Award-winning illustrations.

Balian, L. (1982). *Mother's Mother's Day.* Nashville, TN: Abingdon.

As the mice pay tribute to their mothers on Mother's Day, the relationship among mother, grandmother, great grandmother, and great great grandmother is illustrated. The story holds the attention of preschoolers by keeping them guessing where all the mothers have gone.

Fox, M. (1985). *Wilfred Gordon McDonald Partridge.* New York: Kane/Miller.

This little boy has several elderly friends in an old people's home. They each have different interests and engage in different activities with Wilfred. When he finds out that his best old friend has "lost her memory," he tries to find out what a memory is. He brings her objects that represent his memories and they bring back the old woman's memories, too.

Hedderwick, M. (1985). *Katie Morag and the two grandmothers.* Boston: Little, Brown.

In this British Isles story, a little girl has two grandmothers who are very different. One grandmother is very sophisticated and dainty, the other weathered and hardy. She appreciates them both and even helps them to appreciate each other.

Hest, A. (1986). *The purple coat.* New York: Four Winds Press.

Every year Gabrielle gets a new coat from her grandfather the tailor who works in the big city. She wants a different sort of coat this year. Her mother is not so sure, until grandfather reminds her that she once wanted a different kind of coat, too. Good for K-3rd graders.

Johnson, A. (1989). *Tell me a story, Mama.* New York: Orchard Books.

A Black mother tells stories to her daughter about when she was little and about what her mother did and said. Obviously, the little girl loves to hear this "oral history." Like any young child she knows all the bedtime stories well and enjoys the ritual of hearing them over and over.

Jonas, A. (1982). *When you were a baby.* New York: Greenwillow.

This book lets preschoolers know how much they have grown by reminding them of the things they could not do as a baby that they can do now. It is a good book to start discussions about growing from babies to toddlers to preschoolers.

Kross, S. (1986). *Annie's four grannies.* New York: Holiday House.

A child with divorced and remarried parents has her four grandmothers to her birthday party. When the grandmothers cannot get along, she has to help.

Little, L. (1988). *Children of long ago.* New York: Philomel.

Poems reflect the universal joys of childhood, like going barefoot and jumping ditches. The book also shows things that were different about growing up long ago. The illustrations are of Black rural families.

Martin, B., Jr. (1963). *David was mad.* New York: Holt, Rinehart & Winston.

Like all young children, David has much to learn about his feelings. Here he learns about being mad.

Omerod, J. (1986). *Just like me.* New York: Lothrop, Lee & Shepard.

A little girl has trouble believing Granny, who says baby brother is just like his sister. The baby is bald with pink ears, and he makes a mess when he eats. Granny helps the girl understand that she used to behave and look like her brother and that he will grow up just as she has. This book is meant for the youngest book readers.

Rylant, C. (1982). *When I was young in the mountains.* New York: Dutton.

This story transports you back in time to when the narrator was growing up in Appalachia. Grandparents lived with the family and took active roles. Grandfather worked as a coal miner and Grandmother took care of the family and things at home, including chopping wood and killing snakes. Good discussion starter for elementary school children.

Schwartz, A. (1987). *Oma and Bobo.* New York: Bradbury.

This family consists of the child, mother, and grandmother. Grandmother Oma takes care of the household. She does not want a dog messing up the house; so when Alice gets a dog, Oma pouts and complains. However, the stern grandmother secretly helps her granddaughter train the dog and win a prize.

Showers, P. (1978). *Me and my family tree.* New York: Crowell.

This Let's-Read-and-Find-Out Science Book gives children information on genealogy, introducing the relationships between generations through one child's family tree. Younger children can find out about the relationships through the story of this child; older children can get more information about genetics and heredity in the back of the book.

Stevenson, J. (1983). *What's under my bed?* New York: Greenwillow.

The children visiting their grandfather find they cannot sleep. When Grandpa realizes they are frightened, he shares his own experience as a child visiting his grandparents. Grandpa's humorous story eases the children's fears.

Stoltz, M. (1988). *Storm in the night.* New York: Harper & Row.

The Black boy in this story has a hard time believing that at one time his grandfather was really a boy like him. He learns a lot by listening to his grandfather's stories. One stormy night he learns that his grandfather had similar fears and feelings when he was a boy. Use the wonderful illustrations to maintain younger children's attention.

Watanabe, S. (1988). *It's my birthday.* New York: Philomel.

Bear receives a photo album from his grandparents for his birthday. They review his old snapshots and talk about future ones. Bear sees how he has grown up and the part his parents and grandparents have played in helping him grow. For preschoolers and kindergartners.

Films and videos

Add and Mabel's Punkin Center. (1982). Kane-Lewis Productions, 811 Enderby Dr., Alexandria, VA 22302. 15 min. Color. 16mm

Add and Mabel show how their Punkin Center, a general store, was the hub of the activities in the community at one time. These two older people are at the core of that store, which is now a folk museum. Children will see how an older generation lived and hear the interesting history they can tell.

Anna and Bella. (1986). Direct Cinema Limited, P.O. Box 69799, Los Angeles, CA 90069. 8 min. Color. 16mm

Two elderly sisters review their family album, remembering their past together. This short animated film allows children to see that older people were once young also.

Arthur and Lillie. (1976). National Audio Visual Center. Pyramid Films, Box 1048, Santa Monica, CA 90406. 30 min. 16mm

Arthur and Lillie Mayer recall early Hollywood, the stars and publicity stunts. This octogenarian couple also talk about their current involvement with young students.

At 99. (1974). Visual Aids Service, University of Illinois, 1352 S. Oak St., Champaign, IL 61820. 24 min. Color. 16mm

Louise Tandy March shows that a 99-year-old can be active and happy. She plays the piano, entertains at a senior citizen center, and practices yoga.

Being a Joines: A life in the Brushy Mountains. (1988). Davenport Films, RR1, Box 527, Delaplane, VA 22025. 55 min. 16mm or VHS, BETA, and ¾" video.

A traditional storyteller from North Carolina tells his personal history. The film shows the family values, which have helped the family in difficulties. Use with third graders. Study guide also available.

Death of a gandy dancer. (1977). Learning Corporation of America, 108 Wilmot Rd., Deerfield, IL 60015. 26 min. Color. 16 mm

A grandfather remembers and tells about his days of being a gandy dancer, a laborer in a railroad section gang. The grandson remembers him after he dies.

Growing up — Growing older. (undated). Modern Talking Pictures, Scheduling Dept., 5000 Park St. North, St. Petersburg, FL 33709. Three 15-minute film vignettes on one reel in 16mm, three ½" VHS tapes

Free loan. Films are meant to be used as "trigger films" to begin discussions with children ages 9–11 and older volunteers. Discussion topics for the three films are similarities in growing up, changes and feelings that old and young share, and the universal need for friends. Includes discussion guide.

Luther Metke at 94. (1980). New Day Films, P.O. Box 315, Franklin Lakes, NJ 07417. 27 min. Color. 16mm

An active man is shown building a hexagonal log cabin he designed. The film reviews his life with bits of his poetry, portions of his past, his interactions with others, and his reflections on life.

Never give up — Imogen Cunningham. (1975). University of Michigan, Audio Visual Education Center, 416 Fourth St., Ann Arbor, MI 48109. 28 min. 16mm

Well-known portrait photographer at age 92 demonstrates her long and full life.

Exposing children to an unbiased look at the diversity of old people

The specialness of intergenerational relationships shines through in these materials. Even when an elder is grieving, blind, incoherent, or from a different culture, children find ways to interact positively with them.

Children's books

Buckley, H. (1959). *Grandfather and I.* New York: Lothrop, Lee & Shepard.

This book shows how Grandfather is different from everyone else in the family. He follows the child's lead and they "take just as long as they like" looking at trains and bugs, and whatever else interests them. Preschool–Kindergarten.

Buckley, H. (1961). *Grandmother and I.* New York: Lothrop, Lee & Shepard.

Grandmother is always there when you need her. If you are sick or frightened or just want to think, Grandma's lap is the place to be. Again the book shows a grandparent being especially sensitive to a child. Preschool–Kindergarten.

Casely, J. (1986). *When Grandpa came to stay.* New York: Greenwillow.

A Yiddish widower introduces his traditions to his grandson Benny. Benny enjoys his grandfather until

he sees him grieving for his wife. He says he doesn't like his grandfather anymore. However, Grandpa understands and the two begin to deal with Grandma's death together. They take a flower to plant at the cemetery and then they have a picnic there.

de Paolo, T. (1973). *Nana upstairs and Nana downstairs.* New York: Putnam.

Tommy has a special relationship with his great grandmother (Nana upstairs), who is cared for by his grandmother (Nana downstairs). Nana upstairs and Tommy have a routine whenever he visits. She eventually dies, but he never forgets her.

de Paolo, T. (1981). *Now one foot, now the other.* New York: Putnam.

Grandfather Bob and Bobby have some rituals. When Bob has a stroke, Bobby is confused until he figures out how to continue the rituals with a little variation. Their relationship continues to be special.

Greenfield, E. (1988). *Grandpa's face.* New York: Philomel.

Grandpa is an actor who often has "talk-walks" with his granddaughter. One day the little girl sees him practicing a terrible character and she worries that he might act that mean with her one day. When she tests him to the limit, she finds he remains the loving man she knows. This book has Black characters. Preschool–Kindergarten.

Griffith, H. (1986). *Georgia music.* New York: Greenwillow.

Janetta, a city girl, develops a relationship with her rural grandfather. She shares a summer with him in the country, working in the garden, listening to the birds, and enjoying his humor and music. The second summer he must go back with Janetta and her mother because he is sick. He becomes very depressed, but Janetta finds a way to stir his humor again.

Nelson, V. (1988). *Always Gramma.* New York: Putnam.

A girl and her grandmother sing together, fly kites, talk about nature, go barefoot in the creek, and make a pet cemetery. Gramma starts to change and forget things. The girl learns to adjust to the way her grandmother acts and continues to have a very special relationship with her.

Oxenbury, H. (1984). *Grandma and Grandpa.* New York: Dial.

A visit to Grandma and Grandpa's keeps a child busy. This book for young children reveals the special relationship with grandparents. Preschool appropriate.

Pearson, S. (1987). *Happy birthday Grampie.* New York: Dial.

This Swedish grandfather is blind and has forgotten English. His granddaughter remembers when he used to speak English and she makes him a birthday card with a message he can read with his fingers. When he figures out that the message is "I love you, Grampie," he says in English "I love you, too."

Pogrebin, L. (1987). My Grandma. In C. Cerf (Ed.), *Free to be . . . a family* (pp. 52–56). New York: Bantam.

This is the story of a girl who is embarrassed by her Yiddish grandmother. Then her school begins an oral history project and her grandmother tells an amazing life story to the school. The girl realizes she had a grandmother to be proud of.

Williams, V. (1982). *A chair for Mother.* New York: Greenwillow.

A child, her mother, and her grandmother are saving money for a chair after a fire. Each family member has her own reason to want a chair. They share in making their dream come true. Simple story for preschool and kindergarten children.

Films and videos

Bubby. (1966). Youth Film Distribution Center, 43 W. 16th St., New York, NY 10011. 5 min. B & W. 16mm

An 18-year-old and his grandmother have a warm and loving relationship.

Close harmony — an intergenerational chorus. (1981). Arlene Symons, c/o OCTAVES, 1490 E. 22nd St., Brooklyn, NY 11210. 30 min. Color. 16mm

This film is about elementary students and older adults in a senior day care center who form a chorus together.

Greene Valley grandparents. (1972). University of California, Extension Media Center, Berkeley, CA 94720. 10 min. B & W. 16mm

Documents the foster grandparent program and the feeling of love the children and volunteers share. The volunteers comment on what helping these needy children means to them.

Sunshine's on the way. (1980). Learning Corporation of America, 108 Wilmot Rd., Deerfield, IL 60015. 30 min. Color. 16mm

A 15-year-old working in a nursing home helps the residents form a jazz band. When a great jazz trombonist has a stroke, the girl encourages him to give her lessons and to lead the band. Consequently, the band gets on stage.

The violin. (1973). Attn: Customer Service Department, George Pastic, Learning Corporation of America, 1350 Avenue of the Americas, New York, NY 10019. 25 min. Color. 16 mm

A young boy wants to learn to play the violin. He and an elderly violin player develop a special relationship.

Guides for choosing materials

Helpful guides for selecting and evaluating materials for your curriculum.

American Association of Retired Persons. (1986). *Truth about aging: Guidelines for accurate communications.* Washington, DC: Author.

This pamphlet discussing ageism was developed as a guide for media presentation of older persons.

Center for Understanding Aging. (1990). *Annotated bibliography and resources for education.* Framingham, MA: Framingham State College, Center for Understanding Aging.

Lists materials for developing and implementing curriculum on aging from preschool to adult levels. Updated regularly.

Council on Interracial Books for Children. (1980). *Guidelines for selecting bias-free textbooks and storybooks.* New York: Author.

Derman-Sparks, L. (1989). *Anti-bias curriculum: Tools for empowering young children.* Washington, DC: NAEYC.

Helpful in understanding development of and prevention of bias in children. Resource section includes a number of children's books involving grandparents.

England, C., & Fasick, A. (1987). *ChildView: Evaluating and reviewing materials for children.* Littleton, CO: Libraries Unlimited.

This book has helpful information on selecting and using many types of materials including books, films, and computer software.

The Ethel Percy Andrus Gerontology Center. (1977). *About aging: A catalog of films.* Los Angeles: The Ethel Percy Andrus Gerontology Center, University of Southern California.

Generations Together. (1988). *An overview of curricula on aging and intergenerational programming for preschool to grade 12: An annotated bibliography.* Pittsburgh: Author.

Jantz, R. K., Seefeldt, C., Serock, K., & Cunningham, J. (1978). *The portrayal of the elderly on children's television programming.* College Park, MD: University of Maryland. (ERIC Document Reproduction Service No. ED 173 609)

A report of a research project on the portrayal of the elderly on television.

Jalongo, M.R. (1983). Using crisis-oriented books with young children. *Young Children,* 38(5), 29–36.

Advice on using bibliotherapy with children.

Krogh, S., & Lamme, L. (1985). But what about sharing? Children's literature and moral development. *Young Children,* 40(4), 48–51.

Helpful article in understanding how to use books to present social issues.

Nuessel, F. (1989). Ageism and language. *Linkages,* 3(1), 6–7.

Discusses common language that reflects ageism.

Rudman, M. (1976). *Children's literature: An issues approach.* Lexington, MA: D. C. Heath.

Includes information on selecting and discussing books on many issues important to young children. One chapter deals with issues of death and old age.

Seefeldt, C., Serock, K., Galper, A., & Jantz, R. K. (1978). The coming of age in children's literature. *Childhood Education, 4, 123–138.*

Shelton, H. (Ed.). (1989). Bibliography of books for children. Wheaton, MD: Association for Childhood Education International.

Reviews books for children and reference books and periodicals for professionals.

Wilson, J. (1988). *Intergenerational stories for children and youth: A selected annotated bibliography 1980–1988.* Pittsburgh: Generations Together.

Over 135 titles selected for use in curriculum on aging or intergenerational programs for children preschool to grade 12.

Other materials for carrying out curriculum ideas

These materials can help you carry out some of the suggested curriculum from Part One.

Circle time

Sing rhymes about babies and growing, use them with finger-plays, even make them up. Here are some sources of some old favorites, and some you may not have heard of.

Brown, M. (1985). *Hand rhymes.* New York: Dutton.

Includes "Five Little Babies" and "The Caterpillar."

Cromwell, L., & Hibner, D. (1988). *Finger frolics: Fingerplays for young children* (rev. ed.). Partner Press, Box 124, Livonia, MI 48152.

Over 200 original fingerplays for a wide range of topics.

Glazer, T. (1973). *Eye Winker, Tom Tinker, Chin Chopper: Fifty musical fingerplays.* Garden City, NY: Doubleday.

Includes "Grandma's Spectacles," "Hush Little Baby," "What Will We Do With the Baby-o?" with piano arrangements and guitar chords.

High Scope Press. (1988). *Movement plus rhymes, songs, and singing games.* Ypsilanti, MI: Author.

Teachers' activity book.

Milne, A. A. (1927). *Now we are six.* New York: Dutton.

Classic book of poetry includes "The End."

The real Mother Goose. (1944). Chicago: Rand McNally.

Classic nursery rhymes include many about babyhood.

Activities for young and old to do together

When volunteers visit the classroom you can stimulate activities and discussions by supplying materials that are interesting to the children and familiar in some way to the elders. Many of these materials might be supplied by volunteers.

Dover Publications

1,001 advertising cuts from the twenties and thirties. Dover Publications #25490-9Pa.

Children and elders can look at and discuss the fashions, education, and entertainment found in advertising clips. Elders may remember stories or bring in old items similar to those advertised.

Collectible toys and games of the twenties and thirties from Sears, Roebuck and Co. catalogs. Dover Publications #25827-0Pa.

Includes over 1,000 toys and games as they appeared in the Sears catalog in the twenties and thirties. Children will find toys similar to and different from their own to talk about with the volunteers. Volunteers may bring in old toys or the

65

class might go to a local museum to view old-fashioned toys.

Collectible dolls and accessories of the twenties and thirties from Sears, Roebuck and Co. catalogs. Dover Publications #25107-1Pa.

Illustrations and descriptions of antique dolls, teddy bears, dollhouses, and other accessories can involve children and volunteers in discussions and demonstrations.

Follow my fancy: The book of jacks and jack games. Dover Publications #22081-8Pa.

The long-lived game of jacks is described in many variations. Which way do the children play? Do the volunteers remember playing? The two can learn a new variation together.

Reproduction paper dolls, baseball cards, comic strips, and postcards to stimulate discussion and sharing can also be ordered from Dover Publications. Order their catalog for further information. Dover Publications, Inc., 31 E. Second St., Mineola, NY 11501.

Other sources of good activities

Learning Magazine. (1986). *Great ideas from* LEARNING, *Vols. 1 – 3.* Springhouse, PA: Springhouse Corporation.

Teachers share their creative classroom activities. Volunteers could organize and carry out many of these activities with individual children or small groups. More activities can be found in issues of *Learning Magazine.*

Raines, S., & Canady, R. (1989). *Story S-t-r-e-t-c-h-e-r-s: Activities to expand children's books.* Mt. Rainier, MD: Gryphon House.

Ideas to follow up on stories. Volunteers may like to plan and carry out some of these ideas with the children after reading with them.

Oral history

Many activities will stimulate elders to tell about their past. The following materials can be tools in oral history projects.

Blaustein, R. (1985). *Golden days: An oral history guide.* Johnson City: Center for Appalachian Studies and Services, East Tennessee State University.

Student guide to collecting folklore and family history. Intended for older children, but has been used with gifted third graders and may be adapted for younger children. To order a free copy, write: Center for Appalachian Studies and Services, Box 19180A, East Tennessee University, Johnson City, TN 37614-0002.

Chirinian, H. (1989). *Visiting Grandma: An activity book that's fun for you and Grandma. Visiting Grandpa: An activity book that's fun for you and Grandpa.* New York: Warner Juvenile Books.

These activity books include mazes and coloring activities to do with grandparents. Many of the activities are geared toward gathering some oral history from grandparents. For example, the child asks Grandma what was the worst thing she did as a child. Then there is a space for the child to draw a picture of it.

Davenport, T. *From the Brothers Grimm newsletter.* Davenport Films, RR1, Box 527, Delaplane, VA 22025.

Newsletter includes articles on oral history, storytelling, and film-making. Write for listing of available reprints.

Hands On [Newsletter]. Foxfire Fund, P.O. Box B, Rabun Gap, GA 30568.

Exchange newsletter for teachers involved in Foxfire-type projects. Includes resource and articles. Back issues available.

Oral History Association. *Oral History Review,* 1098 Broxton Ave., #720, Los Angeles, CA 90024.

Teachers and others involved in oral history projects exchange academic and program information. Book and media reviews included in the publication.

Wigginton, D. (Ed.). *The Foxfire book.* Garden City, NY: Anchor Press. Book 1, 1972; Book 2, 1973; Book 3, 1975; Book 4, 1977; Book 5, 1979; Book 6, 1980; Book 7, 1982; Book 8, 1983; Book 9, 1986.

This series of books provides wonderful examples of information that can be gathered in an oral history project. High school students have produced these books by interviewing the rural people of Appalachia. The topics they investigated include toy making, healing arts, gardening, and quilting. The books help students think of questions to ask older people they know.

Foxfire [Film]. (1974). New York: McGraw-Hill. 21 min. Color. 16 mm

Young people interview the Appalachian elderly for the Foxfire project.

APPENDIX
B

Program Development Resources

This section can help you find materials and national resources to develop and maintain your program. Publications, films, videos, organizations, and periodicals are listed to help you understand aging, orient teachers, train volunteers, and organize intergenerational programs.

Included are organizations and publications developed specifically to assist intergenerational programs. The organizations listed are national. Many other organizations in your community may become involved in developing a program. For example, some communities have worked with Kiwanis International, Golden Ring Clubs, Boy Scouts, the Red Cross, the Jewish Council of Women, and State Units on Aging, to name a few. Networking with your local teachers' organization or day care council may give you helpful contacts. It is important to assess your own community resources as well as national resources.

Resources specifically for intergenerational programs

Resource centers

Center for Family Education (Helene Block, coordinator). Oakton Community College, 1600 E. Golf Rd., Des Plaines, IL 60016. 312-635-1461.

College-based program trains people interested in education and gerontology to develop intergenerational programs that will work. Offers the three-credit course Intergenerational Play and Creative Expression.

The Center for Intergenerational Learning (Nancy Henkin, director). Temple University, 1601 N. Broad St., Philadelphia, PA 19122. 215-787-6970.

The center, founded in 1979, has developed model projects. The variety of programs include young and old together in a learning retreat, learning English, and doing improvisational theater; sharing vocational skills; training older adults to be paid child care employees; and involving college students as temporary caregivers to frail elderly people. Publishes *Interchange* newsletter.

Center for Understanding Aging, Inc. (Fran Pratt, director). Framingham State College, Framingham, MA 01701. 508-626-4979.

Center holds annual meeting and sponsors activities to promote better understanding of aging. Center staff available to do presentations and workshops on aging and intergenerational programs.

Publishes quarterly newsletter, *LINKAGES,* for sharing resources, information, and events calendar. Offers other materials and publications.

Elvirita Lewis Foundation, Suite 144, Airport Park Plaza, 255 N. El Cielo Rd., Palm Springs, CA 92262-6914. 619-397-4552.

Organization dedicated to promoting the independence of older people and their active involvement in the community. Publications on aging and intergenerational programs.

Generations Together (Sally Newman, director). University of Pittsburgh, 811 William Pitt Union, Pittsburgh, PA 15260. 412-648-5170.

Conducts research and develops model programs, including Senior Citizen School Volunteer Program, Artist Resource Program, Curriculum on Aging, and Providers of Intergenerational Child Care Program. Staff available for consultation and implementation of Senior Citizen School Volunteer Program. Publishes newsletter, *Generations Together Exchange,* in which intergenerational programs exchange information. Other publications:

Aging awareness: An annotated bibliography (2nd ed.). (1982).

Barrett, D., Myers, R., Kramer, C., & Newman, S. (1986). *Intergenerational volunteer program in special education: A manual for implementation.*

Outlines how Generations Together sets up this program.

Intergenerational stories for children and youth: A selected annotated bibliography, 1980–1988.

Kramer, C., & Newman, S. (1986). *Senior citizen school volunteer program: Manual for implementation.* Albany, NY: Center for the Study of Aging.

This step-by-step manual describes the procedure Generations Together uses to set up Senior Citizen School Volunteer Programs.

An overview of curricula on aging and intergenerational programming for preschool to grade 12: An annotated bibliography.

Share it with the children: Multi-media curriculum package on aging for preschool.

Package contains written lesson and activity plans, motivational and training videotape showing curriculum in action (17 min., ½" VHS), companion guidelines for activities. Components are for sale separately or as a package; videotape also available for rent.

Generations United, c/o Child Welfare League of America, 440 First St., N.W., Suite 310, Washington, DC 20001. 202-638-2952.

National coalition on intergenerational issues and programs. Sponsors a conference. Publishes *Newsline,* a newsletter with information on programs, issues, and conferences.

National Association of Partners in Education, Inc., 601 Wythe St., Suite 200, Alexandria, VA 22314. 703-836-4880.

Association can refer interested teachers to intergenerational program coordinators around the country. Publications and audio-visual materials useful in recruiting and training volunteers and orienting staff in intergenerational programs.

Retired Senior Volunteer Program, 517 N. Segoe Rd., Suite 210, Madison, WI 53705-3108. 608-238-7787.

Publishes *Intergenerational Clearinghouse Newsletter,* which shares program information from around the country.

Publications and materials

Charnow, M. (1989). *Senior center/latchkey manual.* National Council on the Aging, 600 Maryland Ave., West Wing 100, Washington, DC 20024.

Reviews the development and implementation of a National Council on the Aging pilot project in which older volunteers provide an after-school program for school-age children in a senior center. For others to use in setting up a similar program.

Gentle connections [film/video]. Terra Nova Films, 9848 S. Winchester Ave., Chicago, IL 60643. 20 min. 16mm or ¾" and ½" VHS.

Preschool children give hand massages to elderly in nursing homes and day care center. Includes a guide to setting up the program.

71

Guide for replication of "Closing the gap." (1989). Interages, 9411 Connecticut Ave., Kensington, MD 20895.

Guide to assist teachers or activity directors to plan and carry out "Closing the Gap," an intergenerational discussion program in schools. Covers program development, recruitment, class design, recognition, funding, and evaluation. Model was conducted in a high school.

Hegeman, C. (1985). *Child care in long-term care settings.* Foundation for Long Term Care, 194 Washington Ave., Albany, NY 12210.

Overview of six model programs of preschool programs within a long-term facility. Discusses benefits and liabilities of each type, and addresses administrative concerns of the long-term care facility.

Johnson, S., & Siegel, W. (1980). *Bridging generations: A handbook for intergenerational child care.* The Elder Press, The Elvirita Lewis Foundation, Suite 144, Airport Park Plaza, 255 N. El Cielo Rd., Palm Springs, CA 92262-6914.

Describes the founding of a child care center in 1976 by older adults.

Lewis-Kane, M., MacDicken, R., & McCutcheon, P. (1986). *Arts mentor program: A manual for sponsors.* Washington, DC: National Council on the Aging.

This step-by-step manual was developed to assist communities or programs interested in training older artists to teach their crafts to children. Discusses project develop-

ment and coordinator's role, along with all the important issues in implementation.

Murphy, M. B. (1984). *A guide to intergenerational programming.* Washington, DC: National Association of State Units on Aging.

Program descriptions for a variety of intergenerational programs listed by state and subject area. Summarizes programs and lists resources and contacts.

National Council on the Aging (1988). *Program innovations in aging: Vol 12. Planning a family friends project: A working guide.* Washington, DC: Author.

The Family Friends intergenerational model project trains older volunteers to work with chronically ill and disabled children and their families in the child's home. The guidebook is a step-by-step procedure manual for implementing a similar project.

Newman, S., & Brummel, S. (Eds.). (1989). Intergenerational programs: Imperatives, strategies, impacts, trends. *Journal of Children in Contemporary Society, 20(3/4).* New York: Haworth.

Academic book discusses research and issues in intergenerational programming. Useful information for policymakers, researchers, and program coordinators.

Seefeldt, C. (1977). Young and old together. *Children Today, 6(1),* 21–26.

Research on intergenerational programming reviewed.

Seefeldt, C. (1987a). The effects of preschoolers' visits to infirm elders in a nursing home. *The Gerontologist,* 27, 228–232.

Seefeldt, C. (1987b). Intergenerational programs — making them work. *Childhood Education,* 64(1), 14–19.

Seefeldt, C., Jantz, R. K., Bredekamp, S., & Serock, K. (1979a). *Children's attitudes toward the elderly: A curriculum guide.* College Park: University of Maryland. (ERIC Document Reproduction Service No. ED 141 860)

Curriculum on aging based on research on children's attitudes toward the elderly.

Seefeldt, C., Jantz, R. K., Bredekamp, S., & Serock, K. (1979b). *Young and old together: A training manual for intergenerational programs.* College Park: University of Maryland. (ERIC Document Reproduction Service No. PSO 12399)

Guide to setting up intergenerational programs based on research on children's attitudes toward the elderly.

Seefeldt, C., Jantz, R. K., Galper, A., & Serock, K. (1977a). Children's attitudes toward the elderly: Curriculum implications. *Educational Gerontologist,* 2, 301–311.

Seefeldt, C., Jantz, R. K., Galper, A., & Serock, K. (1977b). *Children's attitudes toward the elderly: Curriculum implementation.* College Park, MD: University of Maryland. Unpublished report of research project.

Seefeldt, C., Jantz, R. K., Galper, A., & Serock, K. (1981). Healthy, happy and old: Children learn about the elderly. *Educational Gerontology,* 7, 79–87.

Strutz, K., & Reville, S. (Eds.). (1985). *Growing together: An intergenerational sourcebook.* Washington, DC: American Association of Retired Persons; Palm Springs, CA: The Elvirita Lewis Foundation.

Information on research and program development combined with a directory of program briefs and resources. Also includes a review of annotated bibliographies.

Tice, C., & Warren, B. (1985). *T-LC coordinator's handbook, Teaching-Learning Communities.* Ypsilanti, MI: Eastern Michigan University, Institute for the Study of Children and Families.

Handbook describes the model program, which brings older people and their crafts into the elementary schools.

Ventura-Merkel, C., & Ledoff, L. (1983). *Program innovation in aging: Volume 8. Community planning for intergenerational programming.* Washington, DC: National Council on the Aging.

A step-by-step manual for implementing the NCOA model for intergenerational programs. May be especially useful for programs developed through committees.

What we have [Film]. (1978). University of Michigan, Audio Visual Education Center, 416 Fourth St., Ann Arbor, MI 48109. 32 min. Color. 16mm

Developed by Carol Tice, this film shows volunteers and students interacting in a Teaching-Learning Community intergenerational program. Volunteers teach arts and crafts in a school setting.

Program models

A few examples of the types of programs being implemented around the country. Refer to intergenerational newsletters and source books for more examples and contacts.

AgeLink. Center for Improving Mountain Living, Western Carolina University, Cullowhee, NC 28723. 704-227-7492.

Older volunteers participate in school-age child care sharing their crafts, helping with homework, supervising games, and listening.

Cassette Pals (Linda Harker, field coordinator). Central Branch RSVP, 406B West Ridge Pike, Conshohocken, PA 19428. 215-834-1041.

Cassette tapes are exchanged between children and adolescents and homebound elderly.

Family Friend Program (Miriam Charnow). National Council on the Aging, 600 Maryland Ave., S.W., West Wing 100, Washington, DC 20024. 202-479-1200.

Older volunteers are trained to assist families with severely ill and disabled children by providing activities for the children and support for the parents. The program is currently operating with 500 volunteers in eight sites around the country.

Folk Art Fair (Mary Stamstad). RSVP of Dane County, 540 W.

Olin Ave., Madison, WI 53715. 608-256-5596.

Older craftspeople demonstrate skills, like washing on a washboard and yodelling, and traditional crafts in a school fair. Children participate in hands-on demonstrations with the elders.

Friendship Across the Ages. Campfire, Inc., 4601 Madison Ave., Kansas City, MO 64112. 816-756-1950.

Campfire youth and older volunteers pair up and do activities together for at least six months. Program guide available with information on starting a program and suggested activities. Adaptable to other groups.

Gramma's Day Care Center. Senior Citizens Service, 1750 Madison Ave., Suite 350, Memphis, TN 38104. 901-726-0211.

Infant day care center began employing older workers in 1981; now almost entirely staffed by workers over 55. Program is specially designed to care for children with a high risk of SIDS.

Magic Me (Alfred de la Cuesta, director). 611 Park Ave., Suite 6, Baltimore, MD 21201. 301-837-0900.

In cities across the United States and in Europe, preteens and teenagers learn skills to communicate more effectively with elderly participants in nursing homes through seminars, role play, and interaction. Children provide services and companionship while boosting their own self-esteem and confidence and developing relationships.

Project J.O.Y.: Joining Older and Younger. BANANAS, Inc., 6421 Telegraph Ave., Oakland, CA 94609. 415-655-8945.

Elementary school project involving children visiting nursing home and nursing home residents visiting schools. Intergenerational activities include creative arts, oral history, gardening, and "hands-on" activities. Also intergenerational summer camp, in-depth aging awareness curriculum, teacher training, pen pal program, and par-

ent awareness. Publishes newsletter and handbook. Director available for consultation.

Teaching-Learning Communities (Carol Tice). New Age, Inc., 1212 Roosevelt, Ann Arbor, MI 48104-3905. 313-994-4715.

This model program, in which elders show and demonstrate crafts in elementary schools, has been replicated across the country. Children and elders set their own goals. Handbook available.

Understanding aging

Publications

Asociación Nacional Pro Personas Mayores (1982). *Serving the Hispanic elderly of the United States: A national community service directory.* Los Angeles: Author.

Profiles and lists community agencies, federal organizations, and other agencies serving Hispanic elderly.

Association for Gerontology in Higher Education. *Brief bibliographies* (series). Washington, DC: Author.

Topics currently available: Theology and Aging, the Older Volunteer, American Indian Aging.

Butler, R. (1975). *Why survive? Being old in America.* New York: Harper & Row.

Classic book on aging in America.

Chambré, S. (1987). *Good deeds in old age: Volunteering by the new leisure class.* Lexington, MA: Lexington Books.

Academic book discusses research findings from studies of elderly volunteers, focusing on which elderly people volunteer, what makes them satisfied with volunteering, and what role volunteering has in the life of the elderly.

Dodson, F., & Reuben, P. (1981). *How to grandparent.* New York: Harper & Row.

Practical examples of the role of grandparents, along with child development information.

Dychtwald, K., & Flower, J. (1989). *The age wave.* Los Angeles: Jeremy P. Tarcher, Inc.

Helps the reader understand the changes in our society occurring with changing demographics.

Erikson, J., Erikson, E., & Kivnick, H. (1986). *Vital involvement in old age.* New York: Norton.

Documents the importance of "vital involvement" in old age through a longitudinal study. Discusses stages of human development through the lifespan. Includes revealing interviews with the elderly participants in the study.

Galper, A., Seefeldt, C., Jantz, R. K., & Serock, K. (1980). Children's concepts of age. *International Journal of Aging and Human Development,* 12, 129–157.

Report on children's concepts of age.

Generations Together (1982). *Aging awareness: An annotated bibliography.* Pittsburgh, PA: Author.

Annotations on books and articles on aging, intergenerational volunteer opportunities, schools' role in aging awareness, and literature for adults involving elderly with other generations.

Jantz, R. K., & Seefeldt, C. (1979, March). Oh no! Not me, I'm not getting old! *Life and Health,* pp. 33–39.

Jantz, R. K., Seefeldt, C., Galper, A., & Serock, K. (1976). *Children's attitudes toward the elderly.* College Park: University of Maryland. (ERIC Document Reproduction Service No. ED 142 860)

Jantz, R. K., Seefeldt, C., Galper, A., & Serock, K. (1977). Children's attitudes toward the elderly. *Social Education,* 41, 518–524.

Kaminsky, M. (1984). *The uses of reminiscence: New ways of working with older adults.* New York: Haworth.

Discusses the developmental tasks of aging and the value of reminiscence in accomplishing a life review. Also covers some interesting work being done with the elderly to help them in a life review. Human development theories, facts on aging, and the treatment of the elderly are also touched on.

Kornhaber, A., & Woodward, K. (1981). *Grandparents, grandchildren: The vital connection.* Garden City, NY: Anchor Press/Doubleday.

Discusses the important role grandparents can play in children's lives and the changes in society that affect this important intergenerational contact. Includes interviews with grandchildren and grandparents that were the basis of the study.

Mead, M. (1970). *Culture and commitment.* New York: The American Museum of Natural History.

Insights into societies' views of aging.

Monroe, M., & Rubin, R. (1983). *The challenge of aging: A bibliography.* Littleton, CO: Libraries Unlimited.

Information on books and literature about aging and aging issues. Includes a section on intergenerational relationships.

Quinn, W., & Hughston, G. (Eds.). (1984). *Independent aging: Family and social systems perspectives.* Aspen Systems Corporation, 1600 Research Blvd., Rockville, MD 20850.

Academic book discussing the elderly within the family. Relevant discussions include the meaning and role of grandparenting and the role of children in the lives of the elderly.

Seefeldt, C. (1977). Young and old together. *Children Today, 6*(1), 21–26.

Seefeldt, C. (1982a). Elders' attitudes toward children. *Educational Gerontology, 8,* 493–506.

Seefeldt, C. (1982b). How elders view children. *Children Today, 11*(2), 16–21.

Seefeldt, C. (1982c). Paraguay and the United States: A cross cultural study of children's attitudes toward the elderly. *International Journal of Comparative Sociology, 23*(3), 40–53.

Seefeldt, C. (1984). Children's attitudes toward the elderly: A cross cultural comparison. *International Journal of Aging and Human Development, 19,* 321–330.

Seefeldt, C. (1986a). Children's attitudes toward the elderly in Thailand. *Educational Gerontologist, 12,* 151–158.

Seefeldt, C. (1986b). Children's attitudes toward the elderly in Thailand and the United States: A cross cultural comparison. *The International Journal of Comparative Sociology, 26,* 226–232.

Seefeldt, C., Jantz, R. K., Galper, A., & Serock, K. (1977). Using pictures to assess children's attitudes toward the elderly. *The Gerontologist, 17,* 506–513.

Seefeldt, C., Serock, K., Jantz, R. K., & Galper, A. (1977). As children see old folks. *Today's Education, 66*(2), 70–74.

Seefeldt, C., Jantz, R. K., Bredekamp, S., & Serock, K. (1979). *Elderly persons' attitudes toward children.* College Park: University of Maryland.

Seefeldt, C., & Tafoya, E. (1981). Children's attitudes toward the elderly: Native Alaskan and the mainland United States. *International Journal of Marriage and the Family, 11*(1), 15–24.

Sheppard, H. (1981). *Aging in the eighties: America in transition.* Washington, DC: National Council on the Aging.

Data from a national survey profile trends in aging in America. Includes data on public attitudes toward the elderly, as well as data on housing and income.

White House Conference on Aging (1981). *Older Americans as a growing national resource.* Washington, DC: U.S. Government Printing Office. (GPO-720-019/6886)

Report for policymakers describing existing opportunities for older people and strategies to increase opportunities for involvement in government and the private sector, and as volunteers.

Organizations

These organizations are involved in various ways in studying and helping older Americans. Some produce publications for older people and for those working with them, some do research on aging, some serve as political advocates, and others support programs for the elderly. National organizations are listed, but you will also find information and support from local organizations.

Administration on Aging, Office of Management and Policy, 330 Independence Ave., S.W., Washington, DC 20201. 202-619-0641.

Provides a variety of services and publications for the elderly and those serving the elderly. Assists State Units on Aging with grants and providing a national network.

American Association of Retired Persons, 1909 K St., N.W., Washington, DC 20049. 202-872-4700.

Develops publications and programs to help older people live independently and productively. Publishes *Modern Maturity* magazine and other publications on aging, health, and intergenerational programs. Extensive library with materials on aging.

Asociación Nacional Pro Personas Mayores (National Association for Hispanic Elderly), 2727 W. Sixth St., Suite 270, Los Angeles, CA 90015. 213-487-1922.

Advocates for services for Hispanic elderly. Provides information, resources, and publications.

The Gray Panthers, 311 S. Juniper St., Suite 601, Philadelphia, PA 19107. 215-545-6555.

Organization of young and old working on political and social issues. Publishes *Gray Panthers Network, Health Watch,* and local newsletters. Local chapters choose their own projects. Some have become involved in intergenerational programs.

National Council on the Aging, 600 Maryland Ave., S.W., West Wing 100, Washington, DC 20024. 800-424-9046, 202-479-1200.

Professional organization provides training, conducts research, advocates for the elderly, and publishes numerous materials, including bimonthly *Perspective on Aging.* Publications address issues and facts on aging and program guides for a variety of programs, including intergenerational programs. Extensive library.

National Council on the Black Aging, 1424 K St., N.W., Washington, DC 20005. 202-637-8400.

Advocates for minority elderly and provides information to individuals, groups, and institutions on policy implications for minorities. Publishes *Journal of Minority Aging.*

National Institute on Aging, National Institutes of Health, NIA Information Center, P.O. Box 8057, Gaithersburg, MD 20898-8057. 301-495-3455.

Publishes *The Age Page,* continuing series of fact sheets covering many facets of aging. Available free to individuals and organizations serving the elderly. Some publications available in Spanish or Chinese.

Older Women's League, 730 11th St., N.W., Washington, DC 20001. 202-783-6686.

Advocates for better lives for older women. Publications include reports on the status of older women in society, health care and the elderly, and legislation issues.

Audio-visual media

Teachers who will work with senior volunteers will also need to understand the aging process and the benefits of intergenerational programs. You may want to put together a few written facts about aging and about older volunteers. Generally, orienting staff involves some type of presentation. If you are working with a local program coordinator, a consultant, or with an established volunteer program you may have some help with this part of the program. Audio-visual presentations can help you present information and begin discussions.

Across ages: A new approach to intergenerational learning [Video]. (1980). Temple University Institute on Aging, 1601 N. Broad St., Philadelphia, PA 19122. 28 min. Color. ¾"

Shows the intergenerational learning retreat at Temple University Institute on Aging, emphasizing the benefits of intergenerational programming.

Aging in America: Dignity or despair [Series of three videos]. (undated). Aging, Pacific Presbyterian Medical Center, P.O. Box 7999, San Francisco, CA 94120. 415-923-3440. ½"

Videotape set designed for teaching seminars or leading discussion groups. Speakers on the tapes include well-known men and women in the field.

Generations Together — SCARP [Slide/tape]. (undated). University of Pittsburgh, University Center for Social and Urban Research, 600 A Thackeray Hall, Pittsburgh, PA 15260. 412-624-5470. 7 min.

Explains the Senior Citizen Artists' Resource Program, where older artists share their skills with students and teachers. Provides an introduction on program development and implementation.

Old Mother Goose ain't what she used to be [Video]. (1983). College Avenue Players, 546 Crofton Ave., Oakland, CA 94610. 30 min. Color. ¾" and ½"

A senior theatre group perform an original play depicting the stereotypes of old people in fairy tales. Can help begin a discussion on the presence of stereotypes in classroom materials.

One to one: The generation connection [Film or video]. (1989). Terra Nova Films, 9848 S. Winchester Ave., Chicago, IL 60643. 24 min. 16mm; ¾" and ½".

Teens and elders discuss important issues for society together and come to understand one another better. Viewer's guide available.

Partners in education: Teachers and volunteers [Slide/tape]. (undated). National Association of Partners in Education, Inc., 601 Wythe St., Alexandria, VA 22314. 10 min.

Presents volunteers as partners with the teachers, illustrating benefits to teachers and students.

Triple jeopardy: Hispanic elderly in the United States [Video]. (1981). Los Angeles: Asociación Nacional Pro Personas Mayores. 18 min. ¾″ and ½″

Highlights the special difficulties of the Hispanic elderly.

Working with and training volunteers ──────────

Organizations

Retired Senior Volunteer Program (RSVP), Foster Grandparent Program. Part of ACTION, the federal domestic volunteer program.

Recruitment, orientation, training, and support of volunteers nationwide. Currently involved in a variety of intergenerational activities. RSVP has volunteers in schools, Just Say NO Clubs, and intergenerational library assistance projects. Foster Grandparents give special attention to children in public schools, child care centers, residential facilities, hospitals for sick children, and other sites. Pamphlets and fact sheets available. Contact regional offices for further information.

Region I (Connecticut, Maine, Massachusetts, New Hampshire, Rhode Island, Vermont)
10 Causeway St., Room 473
Boston, MA 02222-1039
617-565-7000

Region II (New Jersey, New York, Puerto Rico, Virgin Islands)
6 World Trade Center
New York, NY 10048-0206
212-466-3481

Region III (Delaware, District of Columbia, Kentucky, Maryland, Ohio, Pennsylvania, Virginia, West Virginia)
U.S. Customs House, Room 108
Second and Chestnut Sts.
Philadelphia, PA 19106-2912
215-597-9972

Region IV (Alabama, Florida, Georgia, Mississippi, North Carolina, South Carolina, Tennessee)
101 Marietta St., N.W.
Suite 1003
Atlanta, GA 30323-2301
404-331-2859

Region V (Illinois, Indiana, Iowa, Michigan, Minnesota, Wisconsin)
10 W. Jackson Blvd.
Sixth Floor
Chicago, IL 60604-3964
312-353-5107

Region VI (Arkansas, Kansas, Louisiana, Missouri, New Mexico, Oklahoma, Texas)
Federal Bldg., Room 6B11
1100 Commerce St.
Dallas, TX 75242-0696
214-767-9494

Region VIII (Colorado, Montana, Nebraska, North Dakota, South

Dakota, Utah, Wyoming)
Executive Tower Bldg.
Suite 2930
1405 Curtis St.
Denver, CO 80202-2349
303-844-2671

Region IX (Arizona, California, Hawaii, Guam, American Samoa, Nevada)
211 Main St., Room 530
San Francisco, CA 94105-1914
415-974-0673

Region X (Alaska, Idaho, Oregon, Washington)
Federal Office Bldg.
Suite 3039
909 First Ave.
Seattle, WA 98174-1103
206-442-1558

American Association for Adult and Continuing Education, 1112 16th St., N.W., Suite 420, Washington, DC 20036. 202-463-6333.

Professional association providing services to adult education professionals, including conferences, seminars, workshops, and speakers bureau. Members can join special units including one for adult educators working with volunteers. Periodicals include *Adult Education Quarterly* (research and theory journal), *Adult Learning* (professional magazine), and *Online With Adult and Continuing Educators* (newsletter for members). Also publishes numerous books, handbooks, and pamphlets to assist adult educators. Sponsors annual national conference.

National Association of Partners in Education, Inc., 601 Wythe St., Suite 200, Alexandria, VA 22314. 703-863-4880.

Provides referrals and information on programs nationwide. A variety of publications and audio-visual materials give guidance to volunteer coordinators and inspiration to volunteers. Publications include: *How To Organize and Manage School Volunteer Programs; Handbook for Teachers; Manual for Developing Intergenerational Programs in Schools; Guidelines for Involving Older School Volunteers.*

Volunteer — National Center for Citizen Involvement, 1111 N. 19th St., Suite 500, Arlington, VA 22209. 703-276-0542.

Membership organization that provides promotional items for volunteer recruitment and recognition. Publications include books, booklets, brochures, and videos on all aspects of volunteer management. Periodicals include *Voluntary Action Leadership,* a quarterly magazine with ideas for volunteer administration, research reports, and book reviews; and *Volunteering,* a bimonthly newsletter for organization members. Sponsors annual national conference.

Publications

Courtenay, B. (Ed.). (undated). *Helping older adults learn.* Glenview, IL: Scott, Foresman.

Booklet provides an overview of the older adult's needs and discusses how to develop, conduct, and evaluate programs for older learners.

Kipps, H. (1984). *Community resources director: A guide to U.S. volunteer organizations and other resource groups, services, training events and courses, and local program models* (2nd ed.). Detroit: Gale Research Co.

Includes a section of resources for the older person. Good for identifying programs by state.

Merriam, S., & Cunningham, P. (Eds.). (1989). *Handbook of adult and continuing education* (7th ed.). San Francisco: AAACE/Jossey-Bass.

Experts from diverse areas of adult education give advice and strategies for trainers in all aspects of program development, management, and evaluation.

National Council on the Aging (1982). *Older volunteers: National survey results.* Washington, DC: Author.

A report on older volunteers summarizes data from five national surveys, showing what type of volunteering older people are doing, who volunteers, and why they volunteer.

Pfeiffer, J. W., & Johns, J. L. (Vols. 1 & 3, 1974; Vol. 10, 1983). *A handbook of structured experiences for human relations training.* San Diego: University Associates Publishers.

Training ideas and information have been used by volunteer coordinators.

Porzel, M. (Comp.). (1987). *Resources for early childhood training: An annotated bibliography.* Washington, DC: NAEYC.

Lists materials used by CDA training programs. Describes books, training manuals, modules, and audio-visual materials.

Training, the Magazine of Human Resources Development. Lakewood Publications, Inc., 50 S. Ninth St., Minneapolis, MN 55402.

Magazine shares ideas and resources for trainers.

Wilson, M. (1976). *The effective management of volunteer programs.* Boulder, CO: Volunteer Management Associates.

Helpful book in understanding volunteerism, the volunteer manager's role, and how to apply research findings in human relations. Includes questions, forms, and worksheets to help plan and evaluate programs.

Woodbury, M. (1985). *Childhood information resources.* Arlington, VA: Information Resources Press.

Includes information on all types of resources for teachers: associations, periodicals, bibliographies, mediaographies, publications, newsletters, and directories.

Training materials _____

These materials can help volunteers understand young children and their role in working with the children. Use them in formal training or make them available to volunteers as resources.

Publications

Granger, R. (1976). *Your child from six to twelve* (DHEW Publication No. OHDS 76-30040). Washington, DC: U. S. Government Printing Office.

Granger, R. (1977). *Your child from one to six* (DHEW Publication No. OHDS 77-30026). Washington, DC: U. S. Government Printing Office.

Basic developmental information and practical advice.

Hendrick, J. (1987). *Why teach? A first look at working with young children.* Washington, DC: NAEYC.

Booklet meant for people thinking about entering the early childhood education field—a good introduction to early childhood programs and teacher responsibilities. It can help you think about what volunteers need to know about early childhood education and how to explain programs and policies.

Merrill, B. (1984). *Learning about teaching from children.* Rochester AEYC, Box 356, Henrietta, NY 14467.

Shows how adults working with preschoolers can better understand the children by observing their play.

Miller, K. (1985). *Ages and stages.* Marshfield, MA: Telshare Publishing.

Covers child development from birth to age eight. Discusses the role of caregivers and gives ideas for appropriate activities.

Riley, S. S. (1984). *How to generate values in young children: Integrity, honesty, individuality, self-confidence, and wisdom.* Washington, DC: NAEYC.

Good examples of home and classroom situations of young children making choices and learning by adults allowing them to be creative and learn by experience. Thoughtful interpretations can give ideas for discussion.

Taylor, D., & Strickland, D. (1986). *Family storybook reading.* Portsmouth, NH: Heinemann.

Introduces the value of reading to children through examples of reading experiences. The descriptions and explanations help the lay person understand how reading develops skills in young children. Also includes a resource section with children's books and magazines.

Audio-visual media

Appropriate curriculum for young children: The role of the teacher [Video]. (undated). Washington, DC: NAEYC. 28 min. ½″ VHS

Illustrates the role of adults in helping children learn in a play-oriented environment.

Beaty, J. J. (undated). *Skills for preschool teachers* [Filmstrip/tape]. McGraw Bookstore,

Elmira College, Elmira, NY 14901.

Series of eight filmstrips with cassette tapes. Because the series is designed for teachers, it covers a broad range of skills, some of which are also important for volunteers.

Curriculum for preschool and kindergarten [Video]. (undated). Washington, DC: NAEYC. 16 min. ½″ VHS

Lilian Katz discusses appropriate curriculum for four- and five-year-olds.

Discipline [Video]. (undated). Washington, DC: NAEYC. 17 min. ½″ VHS

Jimmy Hymes discusses how adults help children become self-disciplined.

Mister Rogers talks with parents [Video]. (undated). Washington, DC: NAEYC. 43 min. ½″ VHS

Mr. Rogers describes some of the pressures on children today.

Partners in education: Teachers and volunteers [Slide/tape]. (undated). Alexandria, VA: National Association of Partners in Education. 10 min.

Shows how teachers and volunteers working together benefit the students.

School volunteerism: An investment for the future [Slide/tape]. (undated). Alexandria, VA: National Association of Partners in Education. 10 min.

Barbara Bush encourages community participation in education and recognizes the contributions of volunteers.

Evaluation tools

Hanusa, B., Marks, R., Newman, S., & Onawala, R. (1988). *Children's view on aging (CVoA).* Pittsburgh, PA: Generations Together, University of Pittsburgh.

Modified children's-view-on-aging questionnaire. Can be administered before and after program implementation.

Mangen, D. J., Bengston, U. L., & Landry, P. H., Jr. (1988). *Measurement of intergenerational relations.* Beverly Hills: Sage Publications.

Example of self-report questionnaire developed for specific program use.

Neugareten, B., Havinghurst, R. J., & Tobin, S. (1961). Life satisfaction index-LIZD. *Journal of Gerontology, 16,* 134–143.

Measurement-of-life-satisfaction questionnaire can be administered to volunteers before and after program implementation.

Osgood, C., Svel, G., & Tahnenbaum, C. (1957). *Semantic differential scale.* Urbana, IL: University of Illinois Press.

Measurement of meaning one feels in life. Administered to volunteers to assess the program's impact on their sense of meaning in life.

Seefeldt, C., Jantz, R. K., Galper, A., & Serock, K. (1976). *The*

84

CATE: Children's Attitudes Toward the Elderly test manual. College Park, MD: University of Maryland. (ERIC Document Reproduction Service No. ED 181 081)

Uses pictures to explore children's attitudes toward the elderly.

Can be administered before and after program implementation.

Seefeldt, C., Jantz, R. K., Galper, A., & Serock, K. (1977). Children's attitudes toward the elderly. *The Gerontologist, 17,* 506–512.

Professional development ─────────────────

Publications

Bredekamp, S. (Ed.). (1987). *Developmentally appropriate practice in early childhood programs serving children from birth through age 8* (exp. ed.). Washington, DC: NAEYC.

Reviews developmental milestones. Discusses appropriate and inappropriate practices in interaction among children and adults; environment; equipment; health, safety, and nutrition; and curriculum.

McCracken, J. B. (Ed.). (1986). *Reducing stress in young children's lives.* Washington, DC: NAEYC.

Helpful in identifying, understanding, and alleviating stress in children's lives. Combines research and practical experience to give teachers important information.

Watkins, K., & Durant, L. (1987). *Daycare: A source book.* New York: Garland.

Lists resources for child care professionals in all aspects of administration and teaching.

Wigginton, E. (1985). *Sometimes a shining moment: The Foxfire experience.* New York: Doubleday.

Editor of the Foxfire Books discusses his project, which exemplifies the belief that the old are invaluable resources for the young. Good resource section and background for teachers interested in the project.

Early childhood organizations

Association for Childhood Education International, 11141 Georgia Ave., Suite 200, Wheaton, MD 20902. 301-942-2443.

Professional organization promoting better conditions and education for children of all ages. Publishes *Childhood Education,* a resource magazine for educators, and *Journal of Research in Childhood Education,* a scholarly journal. Also publishes professional materials, books, and reports.

Children's Defense Fund, 122 C St., N.W., Washington, DC 20036. 202-628-8787.

Advocates for children, especially low-income children, focusing particularly on public policy. Offers annual conference, produces reports and pamphlets on major children's issues of all kinds, and works for supportive government policies.

National Association for the Education of Young Children, 1834 Connecticut Ave., N.W., Washington, DC 20009-5786. 202-232-8777, 800-424-2460.

Publishes *Young Children,* a very readable professional journal, and many books, brochures, and reports, and advocates for quality

education of young children and professional development of educators. Offers large annual national conference.

School-Age Child Care Project, Center for Research on Women, Wellesley College, 828 Washington St., Wellesley, MA 02181. 617-235-0320.

Publishes *School-Age Notes,* a newsletter for providers of school-age care. Conducts research and provides support to child care projects.

References

Ackerman, K. (1988). *Song and dance man.* New York: Knopf.

Berenstain, J., & Berenstain, S. (1986). *The Berenstain Bears and the week at Grandma's.* New York: Random House.

Blaustein, R. (1985). *Golden days: An oral history guide.* Johnson City: Center for Appalachian Studies and Services, East Tennessee State University.

Buckley, H. (1959). *Grandfather and I.* New York: Lothrop, Lee & Shepard.

Close harmony — an intergenerational chorus [Film]. (1981). Arlene Symons, c/o OCTAVES, 1429 E. 22nd St., Brooklyn, NY 11210.

Death of a gandy dancer. (1977). Learning Corporation of America, 108 Wilmot Rd., Deerfield, IL 60015.

Derman-Sparks, L. (1989). *Anti-bias curriculum: Tools for empowering young children.* Washington, DC: NAEYC.

Erikson, J., Erikson, E., & Kivnick, H. (1986). *Vital involvement in old age.* New York: Norton.

Fox, M. (1985). *Wilfred Gordon McDonald Partridge.* New York: Kane/Miller.

Galper, A., Jantz, R. K., Seefeldt, C., & Serock, K. (1981). The child's concept of age and aging. *International Journal of Aging and Human Development, 12.*

Griffith, H. (1986). *Georgia music.* New York: Greenwillow.

Guy, R. (1981). *Mother Crocodile* (translated and adapted from Birago Diop's story "Maman-Caiman"). New York: Delacorte.

Hurd, E. (1982). *I dance in my red pajamas.* New York: Harper & Row.

Hutchins, P. (1971). *Titch.* New York: Macmillan.

Hutchins, P. (1983). *You'll soon grow into them.* New York: Greenwillow.

Jalongo, M. R. (1983). Using crisis-oriented books with young children. *Young Children, 38*(5), 29–36.

Jantz, R. K., Seefeldt, C., Galper, A., & Serock, K. (1976). *Children's attitudes toward the elderly.* College Park: University of Maryland. (ERIC Document Reproduction Service No. ED 142 860)

Jonas, A. (1982). *When you were a baby.* New York: Greenwillow.

Krauss, R. (1947). *The growing story.* New York: Harper & Brothers.

Kross, S. (1986). *Annie's four grannies.* New York: Holiday House.

Little, L. (1988). *Children of long ago.* New York: Philomel.

Martin, B., Jr. (1963). *David was mad.* New York: Holt, Rinehart & Winston.

Mead, M. (1970). *Culture and commitment.* New York: The American Museum of Natural History.

Milne, A. A. (1927). *Now we are six.* New York: Dutton.

Nuessel, F. (1989). Ageism and language. *Linkages, 3,* 1, 6–7.

Oxenbury, H. (1984). *Grandma and Grandpa.* New York: Dial.

Pearson, S. (1987). *Happy birthday Grampie.* New York: Dial.

Schwartz, A. (1987). *Oma and Bobo.* New York; Bradbury.

Spier, P. (1980). *People.* New York: Doubleday.

Stoltz, M. (1988). *Storm in the night.* New York: Harper & Row.

Watanabe, S. (1988). *It's my birthday.* New York: Philomel.

Wigginton, D. (Ed.). (1980). *The Foxfire book* (book 6). Garden City, NY: Anchor Press.

Zolotow, C. (1984). *I know a lady.* New York: Greenwillow.

Information About NAEYC

NAEYC is...

... a membership-supported organization of people committed to fostering the growth and development of children from birth through age eight. Membership is open to all who share a desire to serve and act on behalf of the needs and rights of young children.

NAEYC provides...

... educational services and resources to adults who work with and for children, including

- *Young Children, the* journal for early childhood educators
- **Books, posters, brochures, and videos** to expand your knowledge and commitment to young children, with topics including infants, curriculum, research, discipline, teacher education, and parent involvement
- An **Annual Conference** that brings people from all over the country to share their expertise and advocate on behalf of children and families

- **Week of the Young Child** celebrations sponsored by NAEYC Affiliate Groups across the nation to call public attention to the needs and rights of children and families
- **Insurance plans** for individuals and programs
- **Public affairs information** for knowledgeable advocacy efforts at all levels of government and through the media
- The **National Academy of Early Childhood Programs,** a voluntary accreditation system for high-quality programs for children
- The **Information Service,** a centralized source of information sharing, distribution, and collaboration

For free information about membership, publications, or other NAEYC services...

... call NAEYC at 202-232-8777 or 800-424-2460 or write to NAEYC, 1834 Connecticut Ave., N.W., Washington, DC 20009-5786.